Real Estate Marketing: Pat's Way

. . . with cherry PITS, match STICKS and ALLIGATORS

by

Pat Stewart and Diane Lepley

Real Estate Marketing: Pat's Way
..with cherry PITS, match STICKS and ALLIGATORS

By

Pat Stewart and Diane Lepley

Published By:

Diamond Books

**To order additional copies of this book or for book publishing information,
or to contact the author:**

Headline Books, Inc., P.O. Box 52, Terra Alta, WV 26764
www.headlinebooks.com, Tel/Fax: 800-570-5951 or 304-789-5951
Email: realestate@headlinebooks.com

ISBN 0929915313

Library of Congress Control Number: 2003112357

PRINTED IN THE UNITED STATES OF AMERICA

DEDICATION

This is dedicated to Tom, beloved son, brother, husband and father, whose terminal illness broke our hearts but brought us closer as we sat at the dining room table in the months after he died August 14, 2002, searching for the right words and photos to share in this book.

THANK YOU

We want to thank all of you who helped us put together these words. To Guy Harry Stewart, who has written the ads every year since Pat Stewart, REALTORS® has been in business, who edited every word and who has always been the secret weapon, to Terry Bishirjian who also reviewed this book and helped get rid of the schmaltz, to Karen Lawson who uncovered all the historical data, helped get the facts correct and who kept the office running, along with Jeff Stewart, when we were off working on this book, to Marian Galeano who struggled with our computerized mistakes, to Catherine Teets who added that professional touch, to all our customers and competitors who kept our creative juices flowing, and to all the members of our family who make getting up in the morning worth it.

Contents

In the beginning…

Playing bridge and drinking coffee with the girls is great fun but doing it for five days in a row is too much of a good thing.

I became a professional house hunter…in 1961—in 1962—in 1963. I saw big houses and small houses, brick houses and frame houses, houses that had been loved and houses that no one cared about. Over those three years, I saw everything in Morgantown, the best little city in America, and still I hadn't found the ideal house for me and my family. What I had found were perfect houses for my friends which I shared with them across the bridge table.

One day, the woman who would become my mentor, Jeannette Dorsey, came to me and said, "You've sold three of my houses, wouldn't you like to get paid for it?" So, on the fifth day of consecutive bridge playing, I decided that while I liked the girls and a good game of cards, there had to be something more.

And that more was real estate.

I was 41 years old, with the perfect husband and three children in school. I was lucky because we didn't depend upon me for the rent. I had the luxury of having time to try to find for my customers what I couldn't find for myself…the perfect home. I quickly discovered that REALTORS® had to work really hard to develop clients and to gain the prospective buyer's trust. Finding a way to distinguish myself from the rest of the real estate community became a never-ending battle, along with my mission to get people into a house they could afford. Every day I tried to remember that no matter how much money my customer had in his or her pocket, the desire was the same, to find a dream house where their family members could live happily ever after.

For the next five years, I learned my trade at the side of my good friend Jeannette. Then one day with a check for a thousand dollars from my daddy and assurances from my husband that I could do it, I opened the front door of my own office, a run-down gas station with concrete floors, hand-me-down furniture and a secretary who didn't need pay, just a chance to get out of the house. On weekends, my teen-age daughter and I bonded by pasting blue floral contact paper on the cracked cement walls. We hoped that the bare-bulbed lighting would be seen as intimate rather than a cover-up for innumerable building sins. For the first time, I was responsible for marketing me. Thus, began my 30-year journey of selling property and learning how to promote my business.

Lucky in love and lucky in resources, I had a spouse who was the Dean of Journalism at West Virginia University and who wrote my advertisements. I had ideas; he made them work. We started with short headlines and modest layouts and, as the business became more profitable, we graduated to graphics and four-color spreads.

…as the business became more profitable, we graduated to graphics and four-color spreads.

As my company's thirtieth year approached, I looked at the things that I had done throughout my career and discovered that my long-time friend and loyal office manager, Karen Lawson, had kept track of advertising and promotions throughout the years. I found that old ideas could be translated into the context of this decade and I began to recycle marketing ideas. It occurred to me that other small business persons, like myself, who weren't lucky enough to be married to a dean of journalism might find this collection usable in their communities.

Thus, this book was born.

I started with my collection of funny real estate stories that I have experienced and heard along the way. I had saved the comical ones because who wants to remember the horror stories that always seem to cost us money. Afterwards, I looked at my compilation of marketing strategies.

The question then became, how could I take my ideas for promotions, advertising, and office gimmicks and provide you with a quick guide to use when the advertising director was screaming for your copy and you had no idea what you were going to feature in the newspaper's weekend real estate section. Having put that ad director on death hold all too many times myself, I know the importance of a speedy response. But what works in Morgantown, may not work in Boston, Daytona, Cleveland or Houston. So you may have to tinker with some of my suggestions. But, as for holidays, Easter is celebrated the same way whether you're in Anchorage or Vegas.

It occurred to me that other small business persons...who weren't lucky enough to be married to a dean of journalism might find this collection usable in their communities.

For that reason, I elected to divide this book into months and special topics with the hope that turning to those specific chapters in this book would shortcut your workload when creating headlines and striking advertisements.

January

You can't sell what you can't find.

Some months, you should think about staying in bed. But not me. I'm always ready to show a home, even if it's snowing and I don't know where the house is. It was a cold January day. I prodded a new customer from out-of-town into the car and headed off in the wrong direction. After many a false start and quite a long time later, I finally recognized my mistake and proceeded to the home my client wished to see. When we arrived, he said, "Lady, I don't know how you sell real estate; you can't even find the houses." To this I replied, "When I find the house, you buy it for you fear I'll never find you another one!" Sage advice. He bought it.

JANUARY, MAKE ROOM FOR THE ICEBERGS

Temperature: BR-R-R-R
Mood of the population: Post-holiday blahs
Real estate climate: Couldn't be worse

All REALTORS® know what they most want in listings: location, location, location, but when it comes to marketing those properties, the most salient factor is weather, weather, weather. We are all victims of the sun. If you can't get the client into the car, it doesn't matter how spiffy the sauna or how trendy the granite counters and painted concrete flooring. For me, the key is finding a way to get Harry and Harriet Homeowner to push away from the fireplace, put on their parkas and ski boots and join me for the 40-yard-dash between homes before we get frostbite. If you don't want to take the entire month of January off in Morgantown, you've got to get creative. Sometimes creativity sprouts in the most unlikely places. Even in hospital rooms. I had been showing a house when I decided, apparently, that I should fall up the concrete stairs. A band aid wasn't the answer. What seemed initially like a scratch, led to seventeen stitches, a raging infection and four days in the sickbay. Some people get flowers when they are sick. During my most recent stay, I got ruby shoes. Before I hear a collective groan from all of you wondering just how perverse my family and friends are, I will explain. My daughter (of floral contact paper fame) and one of my daughters-in-law decided, after I had been convalescing for entirely too many days, that they needed to remind me that "there's no place like home." They headed first to the local K Mart where they bought little girl's Mary Janes, red paint and glitter. Then they got "crafty." Voila— sparkling crimson slippers. They parked them on my food tray table. Nurse after nurse commented on my unusual room decorations. As the jokes kept coming, the ideas began flooding into my brain. Off went my spouse to Lowe's to purchase bricks and yellow and blue paint. Then, he got a little "crafty" and produced yellow bricks covered with big blue diamonds, my business logo. He added them to my bedside table to remind me that I needed to get up and at it, as my Daddy used to say. Just that quickly, I began a new ad campaign…follow Pat's diamond brick road; click your heels and take off to Pat's homes.

THE MAKING OF A PROMOTION

As I shared at the National RELO®'s annual meeting in 2001, we started with the well-known fairy tale and my logo, a diamond shape, and created a Diamond Brick Road, using yellow and blue, on which my customers could travel through the advertisement photos. All of my agents climbed into the recesses of their closets to find amusing footwear. Out came old bridesmaid's slippers, beaten-up tennis shoes, men's tasseled loafers from the 70's, and stiletto heels. One afternoon, my daughter and I painted 26 pairs of shoes red and sprinkled them liberally with red glitter. We lined up dozens of bricks and splashed them yellow and added navy diamond emblems.

Armed with two hefty bags of shoes and a wheel barrow full of bricks, I prepared for the weekly staff meeting by placing the 26 pairs on top of the bricks in the center of the conference table. Seeing me commandeering all this heavy bulk, both of my sons, who made real estate their trade—one as an attorney, the other as an associate broker, came to my rescue, as they have so many times over the years, lugging into the building my newest collection of oddities. Before the staff meeting, my lawyer son, Tom, had scheduled a meeting in that same room. His client howled when he saw the line of shoes and suggested that we were missing the most important ingredient…Mountaineer Army boots. A pair arrived special delivery the following morning. They were promptly painted red and glittered.

Red shoes, red shoes everywhere. My agents wore them to open houses. We left pairs of them on top of yellow bricks at our listed houses. We formed a chorus line and had our shod feet photographed for inclusion in the ad campaign. We made Toto-like gingham baskets filled with slippers, and tigers and bears, oh my. Holidays took on an "Auntie Em" flavor. Ideas flew over the diamond brick road, creating an ad campaign that lasted for an entire year. It culminated in December when we bought large Styrofoam circles and squares, wooden dowels and see-through cellophane paper at a craft store to create giant lollipops. These were placed in big urns at the base of the office Christmas tree, which was adorned with hanging suckers of all sizes and shapes. In that month's ad, parents were invited to bring their toddlers to see the lollipop tree. The kids left with a sucker and a photograph of them by the tree.

Ideas flew over the diamond brick road, creating an ad campaign that lasted for an entire year.

The Ruby Red Slippers Campaign[1]

January: "The Good Witch Wishes You A Magical 2001 Along With Pat's Pros"
(Graphics: The Good Witch waving wand and surrounded by stars)

February: "Home Is Where the Heart Is"
(Graphics: The Tin Man surrounded by hearts)

March: "Let Pat's Pros in Their Ruby Red Shoes Get You Home"
(Graphics: Lots of different people's feet in ruby shoes on the
diamond brick road)

April: "List Your Home Now To Be In Pat's Parade (Every Day in May)"[2]
Cowardly Lion saying "GR-R-R-EAT Homes on the Diamond Brick Road"
(Graphics: Lion plus homes sprinkled on a diamond brick road)

May: "Pat's Pros = Home On the Diamond Brick Road"
(Graphics: Cascading homes on the diamond brick road)

June: "Click Your Heels and Take Off to Pat's Home"
(Graphics: A pair of red slippers with heels together sitting on
diamond brick road)

July: "The Buzz About Town Is Get On the Diamond Brick Road"
(Graphics: Big Bee flying around the diamond brick road)

August: "Follow the Diamond Brick Road To Pat's Homes"
(Graphics: Arrows placed on the diamond brick road)

September: Jeff and Toto Say: "There Are No Places Like Pat's Homes"
(Graphics: Broker and his dog with the diamond brick road)

October: "Witch House Will You Choose On Pat's Diamond Brick Road"
(Graphics: Halloween witch and the diamond brick road)

November: "Be Brainy: Call Us"
(Graphics: The "Brainy" Scarecrow on the diamond brick road)

December: "Hey, Get Your Parents to Come See The Lollipop Tree"
(Graphics: Photo of toddler with message balloon above head)

---

[1] A sample of the ads from this campaign, as well as others from the *Homes and Land of Morgantown*
magazine were reprinted with the publication's permission. Over the years, my ads have been a collaborative
effort with skilled input from Mike and Mickey Nardella and graphics created by Brian Pick.
[2] Another promotion which will be described in the chapter for the month of May

ADAPTATION OF CAMPAIGN FOR NEWSPAPER

In the daily newspaper, you can use the same theme with modified or no graphics. For example, the newspaper ad might read: "Pat's Diamond Brick Road Leads to Homes of Distinction" or "The Diamond Brick Road Leads to (name of housing development)."

JANUARY HEADLINES

1.   Leap into 2004 (leap years)

2.   200___ —It's Your Year!

3.   Pat's Favorite Song
SOLD Lang Syne

4.   Winter Blahs?
Forget ´em

5.   See the Cardinals on the Snow
From this Master Suite

6.   As the bells toll,
Begin anew
Think of others,
And they'll think of you.
Happy New Year!

7.   A new home for a new year

8.   Happy New House

9.   Jumpin' January

10.   Time Has Changed
Time To Buy a Home

11.   It's 200__ Got New Home Urge, Call Pat

12.   SUPER Buys (with graphics of football)

13.   Bounce Back From The Holidays

14.   Pat Says: Resolve To Own Your Own

15.   A Solution To Your New Year's Resolution: Choose One of These

16.   Dial 599-9300 for HAPPINESS

17.   Pat: the Problem Solver for Real Estate

18.   Don't Join the I Could'a Club

19.   Double Your Pleasure
        See and Buy

20.   See Pat For Silver-Lined Clouds

21.   Close In But Far Out

22.   What Do These Houses Have In Common?
        (a swimming pool or whatever common denominator)

23.   Try These For Sighs

24.   Within Your Means

25.   Words Can't Do These Justice

January Advertisements

1. "Neither Hail, Nor Storm Will Keep Pat's Pros From Snagging Your Home"
   (Graphics: Little boy sitting on a stool on a frozen pond with rod and line going through opening in ice with hook snagging a house)

2. "Snow Kidding: Pat Has A Home For You"
   (Graphics: Kids frolicking in snow)

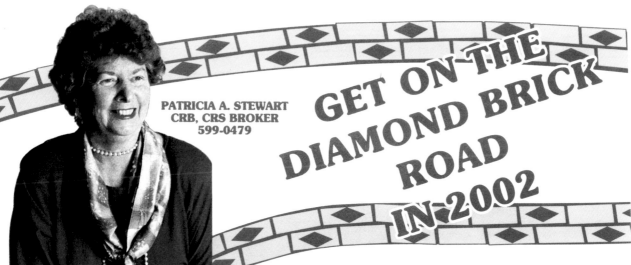

PATRICIA A. STEWART
CRB, CRS BROKER
599-0479

GET ON THE DIAMOND BRICK ROAD IN 2002

GUNJAN OR MARILYN WILL GREET you from this 4 bedroom brick ranch in Downwood Manor. Level house on a level lot is a miracle in this area. $169,900

PAT PRESENTS this 3 bedroom traditional home with Old World charm, hardwood floors, sunken LR & gourmet kitchen. Purchaser may buy an adjoining house. $289,000

SUSAN PRESENTS THIS spacious 4 bedroom home with large kitchen and fenced yard. Located in Suncrest! $129,500

PAT PRESENTS a three bedroom in Old Suncrest with professionally landscaped grounds. $139,000

BEVERLY INTRODUCES THIS well-maintained Suncrest area home. Hardwood floors, double-sided fireplace on main floor, new carpet and walk-in condition. $169,900

MARILYN AND SANDIE SAY nestled among tall trees, this three year old modular offers 3 bedrooms, 2 full baths, large eat-in kitchen and nice decks for your enjoyment. $79,000

ALEX SAYS THE lay of the land is superb - apple trees, outbuildings and barn. Beautiful country home with 73 acres. Only 17 miles from Fairmont. $129,000

BB PROUDLY ANNOUNCES this stately 4 BR home on approximately 5 acres. Lots of room for children to play and located just outside of town. $299,000

BB SAYS THIS IS A GREAT location. Ranch home with lots of decking. The owners have remodeled everything in the home - new roof, kitchen, baths, septic & wiring. $149,000

bruceton bank   EQUAL HOUSING LENDER   Member FDIC

For finance options on all our fine properties....
Call Janet Saul, Loan Originator
at Bruceton Bank 594-2216

Let Pat's Pros in Their Ruby Red Shoes Get You Home

JEFF SAYS THIS HOME IS LOCATED IN THE historical area of South Park. Pocket doors off the DR and walk-up stairs to a finished attic. Hardwood floorsl. $119,900.

PAT SAYS contemporary elegance in Harewood. Home is surrounded by trees for wonderful privacy. Cathedral ceiling in LR, two fireplaces & established grounds. $229,000.

LA RUE PRESENTS THIS handsome buff brick home with off-street 3-car garage & parking in rear. A classic South Park home with spacious rooms and high ceilings. $174,500.

ANNETTE SAYS THE ART NICHES, special lighting & built-ins would showcase a personal art collection as if it were a curated exhibition. Fantastic view of the hills. $269,000.

SANDIE'S RAISED RANCH HAS terrific space with 3 bedrooms, 2 1/2 baths in South Hills. Relax in your hot tub and let the world go by. $124,900.

LISA SAYS CRAFTMANSHIP is the key to this ranch in the Suncrest area. There are 3 bedrooms, 2 baths, family room, outstanding kitchen and established grounds. $98,500.

BILL'S TWO STORY contemporary on 2 city lots has 4 bedrooms, 2 1/2 baths, fireplace in FR and close to WVU campus. $150,000.

AN ELEGANT BRICK COLONIAL IN REEDSVILLE is presented by La Rue. There are 3 BRs, 2 1/2 baths, corner lot, Florida room, 2-car detached garage & beautiful grounds. $149,900.

SUSAN PRESENTS this spacious 4 bedroom split level home. Lots of remodeling and updates. Fenced basketball court on property. $150,000.

DO NOT DRIVE BY SAYS MARILYN, must go in to enjoy! Two bedrooms, 1 1/2 baths, in old Suncrest and grounds are lovely. Hardwood floors for Oriental rugs. $124,900.

TIM PRESENTS THIS beautiful tri-level with 3 BRs, 2.5 baths, two-car attached garage and family room with fireplace. Home is situated on two level lots with view of the mountains. $146,900.

PAT PRESENTS THESE new elegant 2 BR town-homes which overlook Krepp's Park. There are two left. Patio decks & major appliances are included. $115,000.

LA RUE PRESENTS THIS end unit townhome in quiet complex near hospitals, NIOSH & WVU. Woodburning fireplace. Breakfront in LR & bookcase in MBR are handmade & stay. $89,500.

MARILYN SAYS THE glassed sunporch off the LR faces wooded area. There is a stone FP in the living room. Den and walk-in closets. $87,900.

BB PRESENTS THIS 3 bedroom ranch on approximately 1 acre. Private location only minutes from town. New carpet and newly painted. $84,500.

ANNETTE SAYS TO relax and enjoy this maintenance-free three bedroom home. Conveniently located near parks, schools & shopping. Security system installed. $89,900.

ROB SAYS UNIQUE craftsmanship & quality construction. This zero-maintenance home has 3 BRs and 2.5 baths & all on a large 100x100 lot in a desirable location. $129,500.

LISA IS HONORED TO PRESENT an English country home with 4/5 bedrooms and 3 1/2 baths on nearly two private, wooded acres. $249,900.

LA RUE SAYS THIS IS A delightful family home with 4 bedrooms. The large deck is fenced & adjoins a terraced yard. FR with wet bar features a woodburning fireplace. $119,000.

PAT PRESENTS A commercial building with offices or warehousing availability plus one to two apartments upstairs. Located outside the city limits. $174,900

Home is Where the Heart is!

LA RUE PRESENTS THIS spacious Colonial with a second complete living area on lower level for teens or parents. Main floor is filled with light. $265,000.

BILL'S TWO STORY contemporary on 2 city lots has 4 bedrooms, 2 1/2 baths, fireplace in FR and close to WVU campus. $144,900.

LISA PRESENTS THIS spacious country home on approximately 2 acres surrounded by stately trees with privacy galore. There are 4 to 5 bedrooms and 3 1/2 baths. $244,900.

PAM PRESENTS THIS two-story home with panoramic view from the all-around deck. 40+ acres, large outbuilding for shop or convert to a barn. $195,000.

PAT SAYS contemporary elegance in Harewood. Home is surrounded by trees for wonderful privacy. Cathedral ceiling in LR, two fireplaces & established grounds. $215,000.

BEVERLY PRESENTS THIS beautiful new 3 BR home. The natural light and vaulted ceilings give a sense of openness. Kitchen flows into breakfast room with access to deck. $199,900.

LA RUE PRESENTS THIS CLASSIC Colonial with FR or bedroom and bath on main level. Newly painted. Large LR, FP & custom corner cupboards in DR. Fenced, level yard. $144,900.

TIM PRESENTS THIS beautiful tri-level with 3 BRs, 2.5 baths, two-car attached garage and FR with FP. Home is situated on two level lots with view of the mountains. $146,900.

12.77 Acres
$495,000
Stewartstown
Road

SANDIE'S RAISED RANCH HAS terrific space with 3 bedrooms, 2 1/2 baths in South Hills. Relax in your hot tub and let the world go by. $124,900.

BB PRESENTS THIS 4 BR house situated on 61.12 acres with approximately 30 acres wooded - all fenced. House needs rewired, plumbing & drywall. Great hunting. $150,000.

BEV PRESENTS THIS well-maintained 3 BR ranch. Situated on an acre+ lot. Partially fenced back yard, hardwood floors & newly remodeled bathroom. $78,000.

ANNETTE SAYS THE VIEW of the hills is fantastic. Special lighting and built-ins would showcase a personal art collection as if it were a curated exhibition. $269,000.

PAM SAYS GOLFING AND BOATING are just a few steps away in this fully furnished Lakeview townhouse. Features cathedral ceilings, two-sided FP & 8x11 bonus room. $145,000.

PAT PRESENTS THESE new elegant two bedroom townhomes which overlook Krepp's Park. There are two patio decks & major appliances are included. $115,000.

SANDIE SAYS THIS NEW construction is perfect for the first time buyer. Finish the basement according to your special needs. Ten foot ceilings in the basement. $123,900.

DO NOT DRIVE BY SAYS MARILYN, must go in to enjoy! Two bedrooms, 1 1/2 baths, in old Suncrest and grounds are lovely. Hardwood floors for Oriental rugs. $121,900.

PAT SAYS LOTS of house for the money. In great shape. Quiet neighborhood. Can move into this 3 BR, 1 1/2 bath home without any work. $57,000.

LISA SAYS CRAFTSMANSHIP is the key to this ranch in the Suncrest area. There are 3 bedrooms, 2 baths, family room, outstanding kitchen and established grounds. $89,900.

Pat ◆ Stewart, REALTORS®

599-9300
800-693-5300

mail: pat@patstewartrealtors.com
Page: www.patstewartrealtors.com

MARILYN PRESENTS THIS two bedroom ranch situated on a level lot. Convenient to town. Full basement. Storage shed on concrete pad. $48,500.

WELLS FARGO | HOME MORTGAGE

Contact:
MICHAEL HART

304-599-2982
1-800-540-7441
PAGER 304-362-2621

PATRICIA A. STEWART
CRB, CRS BROKER
599-0479

13

Witch
House will you choose on Pat's Diamond Brick Road?

LISA PRESENTS THIS spacious country home on approximately 2 acres surrounded by stately trees with privacy galore. There are 4 to 5 bedrooms and 3 1/2 baths. $249,900

ANNETTE SAYS THE VIEW of the hills is fantastic. Special lighting and built-ins would showcase a personal art collection as if it were a curated exhibition. $269,000

PAT SAYS contemporary elegance in Harewood. Home is surrounded by trees for wonderful privacy. Cathedral ceiling in LR, two fireplaces & established grounds. $215,000

PAM PRESENTS THIS two-story home with panoramic view from the all around deck. 40+ acres, large outbuilding for shop or convert to a barn. $242,500

LISA SAYS CRAFTSMANSHIP is the key to this ranch in the Suncrest area. There are 3 bedrooms, 2 baths, family room, outstanding kitchen and established grounds. $95,000

TIM PRESENTS THIS beautiful tri-level with 3 BRs, 2.5 baths, two-car attached garage and family room with fireplace. Home is situated on two level lots with view of the mountains. $146,900

ROB SAYS UNIQUE CRAFTSMANSHIP & QUALITY construction. This zero-maintenance home has 3 bedrooms and 2.5 baths and all on a large 100x100 lot in a desirable location. $129,500

BILL'S TWO STORY contemporary on 2 city lots has 4 bedrooms, 2 1/2 baths, fireplace in family room and close to WVU campus. $144,900

Be Brainy: Call ...Pat Pam Paul Marilyn Annette

Jeff BB Ed Sandie Lisa Tim Bill Bob LaRue Bev

LISA PRESENTS THIS spacious country home on approximately 2 acres surrounded by stately trees with privacy galore. There are 4 to 5 bedrooms and 3 1/2 baths. Halleck Road. $249,900

SANDIE SAYS THIS home was divided into 3 units. Hardwood floors under carpets. Remove the two upstairs kitchens and have two more bedrooms. Historic South Park. $149,000

LISA SAYS CRAFTSMANSHIP is the key to this ranch in the Suncrest area. There are 3 bedrooms, 2 baths, family room, outstanding kitchen and established grounds. $95,000

PAM PRESENTS THIS two-story home with panoramic view from the all around deck. 40+ acres for horses, large outbuilding for shop or convert to a barn. $242,500

LA RUE PRESENTS THIS handsome buff brick home with off-street garage & parking in rear. A classic South Park home with spacious rooms and high ceilings. Perfect for high school age or children. $169,500

LA RUE PRESENTS THIS end unit townhome in quiet complex near hospitals, NIOSH & WVU. Woodburning fireplace. Breakfront in LR & bookcase in MBR are handmade & stay. $85,000

ANNETTE SAYS THE VIEW of the hills is fantastic. Special lighting and built-ins would showcase a personal art collection as if it were a curated exhibition. $269,000

DAVID PRESENTS this 4 bedroom home with oversized garage situated on 0.74 acres. Outbuilding, above-ground pool and just 20 minutes from town. $155,000

BILL'S TWO STORY contemporary on 2 city lots has 4 bedrooms, 2 1/2 baths, fireplace in FR and close to WVU campus. $144,900

BEVERLY PRESENTS THIS beautiful new 3 BR home. The natural light and vaulted ceilings give a sense of openness. Kitchen flows into breakfast room with access to deck. New construction, choose your colors. $199,900

TIM PRESENTS THIS beautiful tri-level with 3 BRs, 2.5 baths, two-car attached garage and FR with FP. Home is situated on two level lots with view of the mountains. Reedsville. $146,900

JEFF SAYS THERE IS SPACE, SPACE, SPACE in this 4 bedroom, 2-story home in South Hills. Perfect home for the growing family. Family room is off kitchen. $214,900.

ANNETTE SAYS NO expense spared on this completely remodeled tri-level in Suncrest. Spectacular master suite with whirlpool tub, new kitchen & large fenced back yard. $198,500.

LISA PRESENTS THIS spacious country home on approximately 2 acres surrounded by stately trees with privacy galore. There are 4 to 5 bedrooms and 3 1/2 baths. $244,900.

BEVERLY PRESENTS THIS beautiful new 3 BR home. The natural light and vaulted ceilings give a sense of openness. Kitchen flows into breakfast room with access to deck. $199,900.

BB SAYS THIS Victorian home on 4.28 acres would make a great bed and breakfast. Great view of the mountains. $125,000.

PAUL SAYS THIS IS A TERRIFIC convenient location. 4 bedrooms including a finished attic. Detached garage. Fenced yard. Level lot with frontage on two streets. $69,000.

ALEX SAYS the original home is currently investment property - 3 apartments. All rented through July, 2001. $97,000.

BILL'S TWO-STORY contemporary on 2 city lots has 4 bedrooms, 2 1/2 baths, fireplace in family room and close to WVU campus. $142,500.

PAM SAYS GOLFING AND BOATING just a few steps away in this fully furnished Lakeview townhouse. Features cathedral ceilings, two-sided fireplace and 8x11 bonus room. $145,000.

DAVID PRESENTS THIS 2 bedroom home in Westover. Oak paneling in living room, cedar-lined closet in master bedroom, electronic air cleaner and humidifier. $79,900.

List your home NOW to be in Pat's Parade (Every Day in May)

GR-R-REAT HOMES
on the
Diamond Brick Road

LA RUE PRESENTS THIS spacious Colonial with a second complete living area on lower level for teens or parents. Main floor is filled with light. $265,000.

PAM PRESENTS THIS two-story home with panoramic view from the all around deck. 40+ acres, large outbuilding for shop or convert to a barn. $195,000.

PAT SAYS THIS modular (never lived in) is on a full foundation. Oversized one-car garage has a one bedroom apartment. Two additional lots may be purchased for $12,000. $87,000.

ANDIE SAYS THIS NEW construction is perfect for the first time buyer. Finish the basement according to your special needs. Ten foot ceilings in the basement. 123,900.

MARILYN PRESENTS THIS two bedroom ranch situated on a level lot. Convenient to town. Full basement. Storage shed on concrete pad. $48,500.

ANNETTE PRESENTS THIS maintenance-free home convenient to schools and hospitals. Custom designed two level decks. $120,000.

Pat ◆ Stewart,
REALTORS®

599-9300
800-693-5300

PATRICIA A. STEWART
CRB, CRS BROKER
599-0479

Email: pat@patstewartrealtors.com
Home Page: www.patstewartrealtors.com

GR-R-REAT PROS

Alex Abbitt	291-2036
Ed Davis	291-3232
Annette Drange	599-0179
Gunjan Gupta	599-7708
David Harki	291-5394
Bill Hendershot	296-5040
Tim Korintus	725-3219
Bob Losh	292-0062
BB Mercure	568-2308
Sandie Overbey	599-7274
Paul Ragland	291-1112
Marilyn Raich	291-4880
Ken Randolph	292-0346
Bev Randolph	292-0346
Martha Raymond	599-2215
Jeff Stewart	598-0101
Pat Stewart	599-0479
Lisa Teba	594-1393
Dick Twigg	292-6113
LaRue Wilson	599-1535
Pam Windon	599-4413

GR-R-REAT LAND

Apartment Site (WVU) - $34,900
Brettwald Lots - $34,000 - $63,000
Chippewa Lake - 170 acres - $170,000
Hunter Ridge Road - 7 1/2 acres - $25,000
Ices Ferry - 2 lots each - $55,000
Greystone - 0.06 acres - $50,000
Mayfield Road - 2 acres - $25,000
Stewartstown Road - 12+ acres - $495,000
Summit - $49,500 - $51,500
Meadowland - $25,000 - $35,000
Twin Oaks Drive - 1/3 - 1/2 acres - $17,500
Rt. 73 - 1.75 acres - $22,500
Rt. 19 Arnettsville - 1.47 acres - $14,900
Rt. 19 South - 1.16 acres - $11,500

The Good Witch wishes you a along with Pat's

BEVERLY PRESENTS THIS beautiful new 3 BR home. The natural light and vaulted ceilings give a sense of openness. Kitchen flows into breakfast room with access to deck. $199,900.

ANNETTE SAYS THE VIEW of the hills is fantastic. Special lighting and built-ins would showcase a personal art collection as if it were a curated exhibition. $269,000.

LA RUE PRESENTS THIS handsome buff brick home with off-street garage & parking in rear. A classic South Park home with spacious rooms and high ceilings. $169,500.

PAM PRESENTS THIS two-story home with panoramic view from the all-around deck. 40+ acres, large outbuilding for shop or convert to a barn. $195,000.

JEFF'S TWO STORY contemporary on 2 city lots has 4 bedrooms, 2 1/2 baths, fireplace in FR and close to WVU campus. $144,900.

DO NOT DRIVE BY SAYS MARILYN, must go in to enjoy! Two bedrooms, 1 1/2 baths, in old Suncrest and grounds are lovely. Hardwood floors for Oriental rugs. $121,900.

INCOME PROPERTIES

3 Apartments
$134,000

Rental
$ 44,000

South Park
$ 25,000

Duplex
$ 49,900

Townhouse
$ 40,000

TIM PRESENTS THIS beautiful tri-level with 3 BRs, 2.5 baths, two-car attached garage and FR with FP. Home is situated on two level lots with view of the mountains. $146,900.

LISA HAS 4+ ACRES, pond, space for horses, 16 x 24 barn. 4 BR, 2 1/2 BA ranch, 3-car garage and a woodburning furnace for $109,500.

DAVID AND ALEX PRESENT THIS three year old home in A-1 condition. Family room on lower level. Programmable thermostat. Lots of storage. $123,900.

LISA PRESENTS THIS spacious country home on approximately 2 acres surrounded by stately trees with privacy galore. There are 4 to 5 bedrooms and 3 1/2 baths. $244,900.

Magical 2001 Pros

BB PRESENTS THIS 4 BR house situated on 61.12 acres with approximately 30 acres wooded, all fenced. House needs rewired, plumbing & drywall. Great hunting. $150,000.

PAT PRESENTS THIS 3 bedroom ranch near both hospitals. Low maintenance, lovely grounds which include a magnificent holly tree. $89,500.

BB PRESENTS THIS 3 bedroom ranch on approximately 1 acre. Private location only minutes from town. New carpet and newly painted. $69,900.

PAM SAYS GOLFING AND BOATING are just a few steps away in this fully furnished Lakeview townhouse. Features cathedral ceilings, two-sided FP & 8x11 bonus room. $145,000.

PAT PRESENTS THIS BRICK RAISED ranch in South Park. Covered back porch with barbeque grill and 3 lots for elbow room. $99,900.

LISA SAYS CRAFTSMANSHIP is the key to this ranch in the Suncrest area. There are 3 bedrooms, 2 baths, family room, outstanding kitchen and established grounds. $89,900.

PAT SAYS LOTS of house for the money. In great shape. Quiet neighborhood. Can move into this 3 BR, 1 1/2 bath home without any work. $59,900.

SANDIE'S RAISED RANCH HAS terrific space with 3 bedrooms, 2 1/2 baths in South Hills. Relax in your hot tub and let the world go by. $124,900. 0

PATRICIA A. STEWART
CRB, CRS BROKER
599-0479

Pat ◆ Stewart,
REALTORS ®

599-9300
800-693-5300

Email: pat@patstewartrealtors.com
Home Page: www.patstewartrealtors.com

George Washington's got nothing on me.

I cannot tell a lie. I served the Assistant Postmaster General of the United States cherry pits for dinner.

My brother-in-law, later a U.S. Postal Rate Commissioner, was traveling with the Assistant Postmaster General on a speaking tour and brought him by my house for supper. It was just one of those days. The office was hopping and I was running out of time. I grocery shopped on the fly, slinging items into my basket and hoping that I'd get home before the guests arrived. Out came my tried and true recipes including one for Black Bing Cherry Gelatin Salad. All I had to do was dump everything into a mold, along with lots of extra Knox packets, and pray that it congealed. Congeal it did. The only problem was that I'd neglected to check the cherries. Pits, of course. Like any good REALTOR®, it was time to convince my company that the dish was central to that evening's party game. He who has the most pits wins. Prize: Another can of Bing cherries…with pits, of course.

February

FEBRUARY IS NOT JUST FOR LOVERS

Temperature: Frigid interrupted by balmy
Mood of the population: Cabin fever
Real estate climate: Good or horrific

Cold weather can begin as early as October in my town. By November, we've settled in to extra padding, the dress code that generally lasts until March or April—with one exception. Every year we seem to have two weeks of warm weather in February. The trick is second-guessing Mother Nature and promoting houses during that 14-day span. What a roulette wheel that is. You have to prepare for extremes—tee shirt nirvana and Zamboni icing. In 2001, I struck the perfect balance.

San Francisco isn't the only place in America that has a trolley. So do we. Perhaps, it was the similarity of terrain that led my town to purchase two new red and green gingerbread trolleys. Actually, they were brought here to promote commerce in a wharf area by the Monongahela River which would love to add a Baltimore or Norfolk flavor to its waterfront. When I first saw the trolleys, I was like a star-struck kid. They were so shiny…and so empty. Perhaps, I could ride right up next to the conductor, whoops, I mean driver. That was the eight-year old coming out in me. Ride I did. Along the way, I imagined my four grandsons, Guy, Brandon, Willie and Troy, hanging on to the car's sides and I decided right then that I just had to have one for the afternoon. What a wonderful way to transport entire families with young children to Sunday open houses and to give the city's newest transportation option an economic boost.

Visions of Truman danced in my head. Why, we'd whistle stop our way across the landscape. We'd make a family outing of it; we'd refresh everyone along the way with food and pithy anecdotes about the city's sites. I joined forces with an insightful loan officer, Janet Saul, at Bruceton Bank and partnered up for the promotion. Word went out. Someone's renting the trolley. Can you do that? The local newspaper, *The Dominion Post*, heard about my plan and reporter Judy Reckert made it her front page feature in the Sunday Real Estate section. Above the fold, stood Janet and I grinning in front of the trolley. Instead of having to list that day's houses only in the classified section, the newspaper featured a description of every one of them next to a colored stop sign labeled with the whistle stop number. The story took up most of the full page. It didn't matter if it was 30° or 70° that day for all to get on board and see my new houses. You can't pay for advertising like that. Now, some of you may be saying right now, "Well, that's all fine and good, Pat, but we don't have any trolleys in my town and I certainly can't see any value in pasting a picture of Truman on my vehicle and planting stop signs in front of my listings. How does this help me?

THE MAKING OF A PROMOTION: TROLLEYS

So, you don't have a trolley. What have you got? C'mon. I'm betting you've got a bus—either commercial or educational, as in the yellow school kind. My guess is you can find someone who's willing to rent you some form of mass transportation. If not a bus, then perhaps an RV or van. The key is to dress up the vehicle with promotional advertising and find a way to make the event fun for the whole family.

It doesn't have to be expensive. In my case, I was lucky to have a bank which presumably saw the event as an opportunity for meeting new clients. It turned out they were right, as several passengers along the way sat down with the loan officer at the bank, the trolley's final stop, to discuss financing. Because my idea was the first of its kind in my community, I got free advertising in the feature story. I gained and the town gained. The trolleys, which had seen little ridership, became the destination for the weekend wedding party or organizations looking for a fun afternoon outing for employees. What began as a wistful reminder of youth blossomed into community service and a whale of a promotion.

RECIPES

A lot of us have been sending out recipes to potential clients. For years, I included a favorite recipe card in my bills and Christmas cards. Some of the recipes were whimsical, like the one for elephant stew calling for two elephants and a heck of a lot of rabbits, while others, like the one for Black Bing Cherry Salad, were ones I swore by when entertaining the masses. The reception for the cards was positive but the cost mounted, as postage costs soared. Recently, I came up with a modification of that theme.

As we've all been told over the years, wafting pleasant smells at an open house helps promote a positive image of the residence. I've boiled potpourri with the best of them. I've baked bread, sprinkled cinnamon, and burned vanilla candles by the truckload. Recently, I decided that I'd try baking a favorite recipe at my open houses and having a stack of that recipe's cards on hand. On the back of each card, I suggest the agent write the date of the opening, the address, and identifying contact information about yourself. Those who visit will have some way to remember you and the house in addition to the information sheet. And, if you don't have any viewers, at least you can leave behind a dish for the homeowner as a pleasant memory of that day which may soften the sting of non-activity. As each month has a theme or flavor, I suggest you tailor your recipe selections to non-messy items which capture the spirit of the month. For example, you might prepare frozen pickles in January, pumpkin bread in October or hearty hot chocolate in November.

OFFICE HAPPINESS PROMOTION

Everybody loves decorations. We used to decorate our homes only for Christmas. Now holiday decorating has become a lucrative cottage industry and every month has something memorable about it whether it's a multitude of snowflakes for January or the more traditional egg at Easter. In February, it's obviously hearts. I've found my staff and agents look forward to the changing of the "look" each month and that it brings a smile to girls and guys alike. In 2002, I strung red heart-shaped cookie cutters on a tree and passed them out to everyone. In March, I fashioned a large basket filled with green- colored items: pot holders, "Kiss Me, I'm Irish" pins, spatulas, shamrock spreaders, sponges, candies, glass marbles and watermelon ball scoops. In June, it was miniature cars; in August, came yard lanterns. You get the idea…fun stuff.

FEBRUARY HEADLINES

1.   Washington Didn't Sleep Here
But You Can

2.   We'll Find You A Home To Love In
Not Just Live In

3.   Honest Abe
These Are Good Buys

4.   Don't Forget Your Valentine
Buy Her a New Home

5.   It's A Sweetheart Deal

6.   Pat's In Love with People in the Morgantown area

7.   Bring Your Valentine to Pat's Pros

8.   Kiss Your Landlord Goodbye

9.   Watch your Wife
Her Eyes Will Light Up
When She Sees These

10.   Dream No More
We've Got Your Home

11.   You Can't Afford
Not To Buy One

12.   Pat Loves Saturdays
Spend the Day With Her

13.   PROCRASTINATION
Don't Be Guilty Of It
Call Us Now

14.   Why I Love Pat
(Question and Answer Ad with Testimonials from buyers)

15.   For Great Homes and Quality Service, Call Pat

16.   Buy A New Home
        Create Happiness

17.   Do the Manor Mix
        (use when you have several homes from one manor)

18.   Listing? You'll Love Pat's Pros
        Selling? You'll Love Them Too
        Buying? They Can't Be Beat

19.   Pat's Horizon Reaches Around the World

20.   You Name The Location And the Diamond Will Be There

21.   Go...See...Buy

22.   Get the Inside Story

23.   Strike It Rich By Buying A Home

24.   Pat Plans to Please
        With One Of These

February Advertisements

1. "She'll be Loving You Al-ways
   When You Buy From Pat's Pros"
   (Graphics: music notes)

2. "The Heart of Pat Stewart Real Estate is Its People"
   (Graphics: photos of agents inside a heart)

3. "Gift Certificate to My Love
   This entitles you to go house hunting. The
   Down-payment is in the bank.
   Signed: _____ "
   (Graphics: shape the ad like a gift certificate with a generous border)

4. "We'll Move Heaven and Earth to Find The Right House For You"
   (Graphics: Agents sitting on tractor)

Get A Home Investment

Where Rent Checks Go

DAVID AND ALEX PRESENT THIS three year old home in A-1 condition. Family room on lower level. Programmable thermostat. Lots of storage. $114,900.

BEV SAYS THIS South Hills home has it all - 6 bedrooms (4 on the main floor), summer kitchen, and in-ground pool. Tastefully decorated. $197,500.

LISA PRESENTS THIS spacious country home on approximately 2 acres surrounded by stately trees with privacy galore. There are 4 to 5 bedrooms and 3 1/2 baths. $224,900.

DO NOT DRIVE BY SAYS MARILYN, must go in to enjoy! Two bedrooms, 1 1/2 baths, in old Suncrest and grounds are lovely. Hardwood floors for your Oriental rugs. $117,900.

ANNETTE OR MARILYN WILL GREET you from this 4 bedroom brick ranch in Downwood Manor. Level house on a level lot is a miracle in this area. $185,000.

SANDIE SAYS GOLFING AND BOATING are just a few steps away in this fully-furnished Lakeview townhouse. Features cathedral ceilings, two-sided FP & 8x11 bonus room. $145,000.

ANNETTE PRESENTS THIS maintenance-free home convenient to schools and hospitals. Custom designed two level decks. $116,000

BEV SAYS THIS Colonial home is situated on one of the largest lots in Oakview. Lot is wooded & private. Unfinished basement allows buyer to create family room or ????. $167,000

SANDIE'S RAISED RANCH has terrific space with 3 bedrooms, 2 1/2 baths in South Hills. Relax in your hot tub and let the world go by. $122,900.

BOB SAYS timeless elegance with view of the valley. There are 9' ceilings, 4-car garage, 5 bedrooms, 4 baths and more. $375,000.

PAT SAYS THE lilacs bloom outside the kitchen window. Brick and aluminum siding home is on a flat lot in an established neighborhood. $89,000.

Today!

PAT PRESENTS THIS 2-story home with panoramic view from the all around deck. 40+ acres, large outbuilding for shop or convert to a barn. $175,000

ANNETTE SAYS THE VIEW of the hills is fantastic. Special lighting and built-ins would showcase a personal art collection as if it were a curated exhibition. $244,000

BEV ASKS DO YOU WANT an older 2-story home with personality? Impossible, not so. This house has been totally redone. Off-street parking & a beautiful finished attic. $110,000

INVENTORY HOT SHEET

PINEVIEW DRIVE - Office building	$ 189,000
BROCKHAVEN ROAD - Office building & apartment	$ 149,900
BRUCETON MILLS - Home and laundromat	$ 134,900
ASHTON AVENUE - Duplex (1/2 rented)	$ 49,900
HOLLAND AVENUE - 3 unit apartment building	$ 95,000
OLD FRAME ROAD - 5 acre ranch + apartment	$ 99,000
HOARD ROAD - 2 Residential homes on 11 acres	$ 450,000
BROCKWAY AVENUE - Duplex	$ 62,500
BEVERLY AVENUE - Lot zoned for 4-plex	$ 34,900

BUILDING LOTS

BRETTWALD - 24 lots available	$34,000 - $ 63,000
MEADOWLAND - 1/2 - 3/4 acres	$25,000 - $ 35,000
ICES FERRY - 2 lots	$50,000 & $ 60,000
KIMBERLY ESTATES - 3 acres	$ 25,000
LAUREL RIDGE DRIVE - Greystone	$ 50,000
MAYFIELD ROAD - 2.6 acres	$ 25,000
RT. 1 BOX 129 - 11.20 acres	$ 44,000
RT. 73 - 1.75 acres	$ 22,500
SUMMIT - 1.44 acres	$ 49,500
SUMMIT - 1.56 acres.	$ 51,500
STEWARTSTOWN ROAD - 12 acres	$ 450,000

PAT'S PROS

Alex Abbitt	291-2036	Paul Ragland	291-1112
Ed Davis	291-3232	Marilyn Raich	291-4880
Annette Drange	599-0179	Ken Randolph	292-0346
Gunjan Gupta	599-7708	Bev Randolph	292-0346
David Harki	291-5394	Martha Raymond	599-2215
Bill Hendershot	296-5040	Jeff Stewart	598-0101
Tim Korintus	725-3219	Pat Stewart	599-0479
Bob Losh	292-0062	Lisa Teba	594-1393
BB Mercure	568-2308	Dick Twigg	292-6113
Sandie Overbey	599-7274	LaRue Wilson	599-1535
		Pam Windon	599-4413

PATRICIA A. STEWART
CRB, CRS BROKER
599-0479

599-9300
800-693-5300

Pat Stewart,
REALTORS®

Email: pat@patstewartrealtors.com
Home Page: www.patstewartrealtors.com

WELLS FARGO HOME MORTGAGE
304-599-2982

It's always improv night at Pat's.

You don't need stand-up comics to headline a celebration at our house. But a good sport sure doesn't hurt. Curve balls are my specialty and innovation is a necessity. Since I sell real estate by day and entertain dignitaries by night, last-minute prep is my norm.

Every year, the West Virginia University "J" School invites well-known correspondents to speak with the students and faculty about their exploits. In 1975, NBC's Tom Brokaw, then the 35-year-old White House Correspondent, was featured and honored at a post-event cocktail party at the Stewart residence. He had just discussed his views on that "pivotal time" when neither the President nor Vice President had been elected, calling them "historical accidents." You would think I would have been preparing for such a special occasion for months. You'd think that. But you'd be wrong.

Instead, I was selling houses. Some erstwhile client had me searching the hills for listings while my saintly husband patiently waited for me to don a gown and make sure there were appropriate set-ups at the bar. That was no problem, but I discovered we had cocktail napkins for Halloween and Thanksgiving, July Fourth and Christmas, but none for a non-holiday affair.

To another faculty wife, I stated, "Save my life, help me!" In she came, with napkins…for a happy birthday. "That's all they had," she responded.

As Tom Brokaw came in the front door, I exclaimed, "happy birthday" and quickly placed wooden match sticks between his fingers which were lit as the crowd sang "Happy Birthday." As the last chord evaporated in the air, Tom Brokaw turned to me and protested, "Why, that's very nice, but it isn't really my birthday." Handing him a drink—and napkin, I informed him. "It is tonight; so, enjoy it!"

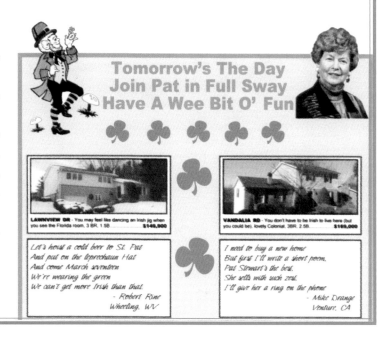

MARCH, MY BIRTHDAY MONTH

Temperature: Crocuses are fighting the occasional snowman for landscape
Mood of the population: Yearning for the Spring wardrobe
Real estate climate: Heating up

I was born on Saint Patrick's Day and my parents took advantage of it. They named me Patricia…Pat. Tartan plaid and Irish kisses have always held a special place in my heart, although I must admit, I've never taken a liking to green beer, or beer of any color for that matter. But I do like to party and the 17th has always seemed like as good a day as any to kick up my heels with my favorite man. Recently, I thought why not make it a double whammy and design a business promotion around it. Thus, a limerick contest was born.

HOW TO RUN A LIMERICK CONTEST

In early March of the first year, I introduced the contest in the local newspaper's classified ads with the opening salvo and instructions:

> *"There once was a REALTOR® named Pat*
> *Who slipped on her Leprechaun hat*
> *And took one and all*
> *To homes big and small*
> *Rolling out the welcoming mat."*

Top of the Day to you. Put on your Irish thinking cap and help Pat CELEBRATE Saint Patrick's Day by submitting your limerick to her via Email: pat@patstewartrealtors.com or by letter. An outside judge will select the best and Pat will print one or more on St. Patrick's Day, March 17. Entries due March 10.

The contest gave everyone a shot at part of his or her 15 minutes of fame and didn't run afoul of our State Real Estate Commission's ban on prizes. The submissions were not limited to stanzas about me. In fact, two of the winning submissions were about other company agents. Once the limericks were selected, the real creativity began. Creating advertisement copy with an Irish flavor was next. The final ad, which follows, was done in green with shamrocks and leprechauns sprinkled in the border and background. The ad featured four limericks and six houses. This whimsical and well-received ad[3] won a national award at the 2003 RELO® convention where it took first place in the Marketing/ Newspaper Advertising Competition for real estate firms of my size.

---

[3] This ad, as well as the 2003 version on this month's cover at page 29 and other samples on next page, were reprinted with the permission of *The Dominion Post*.

AD LAYOUT ON ST. PATRICK'S DAY

Headline: **It's St. Patrick's Day**
Celebrate – Buy Now

Photo of house

Ad copy: You don't have to be Irish
to live here (but you could be); old world
charm, sunken living room, gourmet
kitchen, 3BR,3.5B, price

Photo of house

Ad copy: You may feel like dancing a jig
once you move into this elegant Hopecrest
home, unbelievable master suite, 4BR,
3.5B, price

Limerick in green print

Selling homes was her forte
She'd show 17 in a day!
If Pat couldn't swing it,
She'd probably wing it.
And I hear she is from Gassaway!
—Connie Harwood

Limerick in green print

There once was a woman named "Pat"
Who always chose earrings so that,
Though they jiggled
When she wiggled
They always looked great with a hat.
—Charlotte Nath

Photo of house

Ad copy: You don't have to dress in
green to see this attractive brick ranch,
4BR, 2B, family room, warranty, price

Photo of house

Ad copy: Start a rose garden on these
approx. 6 ac. while you sing "My Wild
Irish Rose." Handsome home, 4BR, price

Limerick in green print

There was a young REALTOR® named Pat
Who could sell a house just like that
She rented a bus
And without a fuss
She rolled out the welcome mat.
—Bernard Schreurs

Limerick in green print

There now is a REALTOR® named Sandie
Her home selling skills are just dandie.
Her craft is a science.
She treasures her clients
She's surely a REALTOR® to keep handy!
—Sandie Overby

Photo of house

Ad copy: You've heard of the Irish
heather—why not live in a townhome on a
Street by that name? Beautiful 2BR, price

Photo of house

Ad copy: You may not find a
leprechaun in the yard., but you'll
enjoy this home, all on one floor
living, price.

Pat Stewart, REALTORS® with address, phone numbers, associations, etc.

One of the submissions had a Halloween theme[4] so we saved it until October due to its content. The week after your contest, you may want to put a rider on your weekly ad thanking everyone who participated in the contest.

Birthdays, not just notorious ones, always present a reason to celebrate or to acknowledge people in your office or in the community. You should keep a list of all of your agents' and staff members' birthdays, as well as those of bankers, builders and other people in the community. Saying happy birthday in an ad to those with birthdays that month is a way to make their day special and for you to say thank you.

---

[4] There once was a REALTOR® named Jeffrey, Who even checked for bats in the belfry, He ran around town, Pounding signs in the ground, And passing plump pumpkins around.

MARCH HEADLINES

1. March into Spring
    With a New Home

2. Shake Off That Wintry Feeling
    House-hunt with us

3. You'll Dance A Jig
    When You Buy One of these

4. No BLARNEY
    These are good buys

5. SHURE and BEGORRAH
    These are dillies

6. Try the Luck of the Irish This Weekend
    It's the Perfect Time To Find the Right Home

7. Sap's A Risin'
    Take Advantage of budding trees, flowering shrubs
    and early flowers in a new home.

8. March + Spring = Home Buying

9. Happiness =
    *Pat's Pros who care about you
    *A New Home this Spring

10. Good-bye Winter
    Hello Spring

11. It's the Season to buy a New Home

12. Put Your Green Thumb to Work
    In This Home's Yard

13. Shake off that Wintry Feeling

14. Get Fresh With Spring

15. Get A Fresh Start in A New Home

16.   Drive Away Those Wintry Blues

17.   Got Buyin' Itch
        Let Pat Scratch It

18.   Solid Value in These Homes

19.   My Oh My – What A Buy!

20.   S-P-R-E-A-D   O-U-T in one of these
        (for large houses or homes with many bedrooms)

21.   Homes Are Selling
        Get On The Bandwagon

22.   For the Good Life, Call Pat

23.   Call Pat's Pros, You'll Become A Believer

24.   Don't Sit Still
        Time To Move

25.   You're A VIP With Us

MARCH Advertisements

1. "Buying? MARCH to Pat's Place"
   (Graphics: Marching feet or marching band)

2. "Spring Into Action
   Call Pat's Pros"
   (Graphics: Take picture of all of your agents with gardening tools in front of
   a new bed of flowers or carrying trays of new plants)

3. Limerick contest ads

Some listings require protective gear.

Just before the bunnies arrive in April, I travel north from vacation land. One year, I stopped along the way to examine three referrals in Florida given to me by the owner of a glass plant in my hometown, one of my very best clients. The properties had been on the market for a while without any bites. Wanting to see what I had referred, I booked a local agent who headed out with me in tow.

We drove and drove and drove…until we reached the listed orange grove. Needing desperately to stretch my legs, I threw open the door and started to jump out of the car. The agent threw his arm across my body and said, "I don't believe I'd do that if I were you. The orchard is full of fire ants and you need special boots to step foot on it." We viewed it from the car.

We drove to property two, picturesque waterfront property surrounding a lake. As we approached, I thought it looked ideal for the next retirement community. Again, I started to get out of the car so I could walk the land. Once more, the agent said, "I don't believe I'd do that. There are certain preparations we must make first." He began to lay on the horn. All the logs around the lake got up and waddled into the water. A gang of University of Florida mascots…alligators. Seeing my contemporaries become moving targets no longer seemed like such a good idea.

Finally, we drove to the third property, a small motel that Anthony Perkins would have been proud of. It was mid-morning, around 10:00 a.m., but we didn't see anyone in the general office. Knocking on the door, we were met by a shot gun-toting manager who screamed, "How dare you bother me this early in the morning!"

Let's review. Special fire ant-repelling boots, a coat of armor, and a bullet-proof vest. I wrote in my Day Planner: Buy protective clothing for my Florida customers.

APRIL: FOR FOOLS, COLORED EGGS AND THE OVERLY TAXED

Temperature: Picture-perfect for crawling in the warm grass hiding chocolate
Mood of the population: Down-right giddy over tossing the jackets
Real estate climate: Looking for a new shelter and shelters

At the first sign of warm breezes in Morgantown, you can see bikini-clad coeds on the pitched roofs all over campus. If nothing else, this energizes the sport of house hunting. Other post-college gals can be seen hanging out their windows trying to remove the salty, icy grime of winter. Ahhhh, spring cleaning. It's a time when homeowners take stock of their surroundings and look to setting up house in newer duds. I love this time of year. Inventory begins to fly off the shelf. It's time to hunt for new listings. HUNT is the watchword for April…whether it's for Easter goodies or tax-saving investments. Helping my agents dust off the winter doldrums and find the newest residential gems is critical for me because I need no less than 30 listings for my annual promotion in May—no skipping ahead. No peeking. More on that later.

THE RABBITS ARE COMING; THE RABBITS ARE COMING.

Sometimes, agents need help putting hops in their steps. In keeping with the monthly theme, I asked one of my closest and dearest friends, Lorraine Owens, to make me some clay rabbits. As usual, she outdid herself, creating 12 lovely delicate creatures which I displayed in a central place in the office. After their appearance had enticed the agents for about a week, I told them at the next staff meeting that each rabbit would find a new home in one of the agent's own houses for each new listing he or she brought in. The rabbit hunt began. Agents scattered to all compass directions — gathering rabbits along the way. Listings begat rabbits. Rabbits begat listings. Rabbits begat rabbits. What started with 12 led to shopping outings galore as I searched for unusual hares. This promotion could be tailored to any month. There's no sanctity to rabbits; it could be zebras…or better yet, ducks.

HELP QUACKIN' MAX SPLASH

In 2003, I looked around for another furry animal and out from a bin fell a foot-high duck with big orange feet whom we named "Quackin' Max." To mystify my agents, I put fliers in each of their mailboxes stating "Quackin' Max is Coming!" I gave no explanation. He remained a mystery for days until he was introduced, along with this year's contest rules,[5] at the first staff meeting after my return North from Florida. With the opening salvo, "A REALTOR® without listings is like a duck out of water," I passed Max around at the meeting while my agents massaged his soft feathery head and examined a new contest board showing three teams with captains. Each agent learned that s/he could "Help Max Splash" by obtaining a new listing which would be designated by waves next to his/her name on the talley poster.

---

[5] A copy of the contest flyer may be found at page 38.

The contest contained incentives for the teams and the individuals. In addition to bragging rights, the winning team would be treated to a group dinner at a fancy restaurant in town. Each individual lister would win a chance for cash and prizes, including Max himself. Calling it "Mad Duckbills," a close kin to mad money, I numbered the bottoms of rubber duckies and prepared envelopes bearing the number corresponding to the duckie and containing a predetermined amount of money. The quantity of Mad Duckbills varied wildly and the amount the lister received was based upon the random drawing of a numbered duckie. The "duckie listers" were announced with much fanfare each week at the staff meeting. After each listing agent for that week selected a rubber duckie, s/he set it afloat in a vessel set up in the reception area. From that office tub, the winning duckie was drawn at the contest's end and the individual lister received a prize. After the contest was announced, ducks began appearing everywhere in the office. I found frilly ducks who just sat, duck puppets that quacked, ducks who sang, even one who danced, and, of course, I purchased all sizes of rubber duckies. I sent a large rubber duckie into the tub before the contest began. Ducks were placed on desks, in bathrooms and in common areas. We hid ducks in the most unusual places; we moved them around so they never stayed in the same places. Every morning my agents played hiding-duck-seek. On the fun scale, I rate this contest: Quack, quack, quack.

EASTER TREASURES

The more fun house hunting is, the more likely we'll get the new listing or new client. People want to get in on eye-catching promotions. April is the perfect time to have your agents dig those treasure chests and Army lockers out of their attics for placement in homes of new listings. Overlaying the Easter theme upon that of the treasure hunt creates a Sunday afternoon for the entire family.

THE MAKING OF A PROMOTION: THE EASTER TREASURE HUNT OF HOUSES

Hunt Recipe
1. Select a variety of various-priced homes.
2. Dig out enough treasure chests to have one per home—placed in the entryway.
3. Buy an assortment of HARD candy—there's nothing worse than chocolate on your client's white furniture. Fill the chests with disposable plastic grocery bags for volume and then cover with vibrant Easter paper. Finally, place the bag of candy in a bowl on top of the lively arrangement. Your imagination is the only limitation to this creation.
4. Decorate those generic brown lunch bags with a sticker of your company's name or logo, your agent's business card or just festive words like "House-hoppity" or "Chocorific residence."
5. Take a map of your town and put Easter eggs on each of the locations for the open houses. Not only can each house-hunter be given a copy of the map at the first house of the hunt but it can also be reproduced in the newspaper.
6. Add the town's populace, young and old alike.

Everybody likes a good Easter egg hunt. This one has the advantage of entertaining the kids while Mom and Dad check out the Master suite.

A REALTOR® WITHOUT LISTINGS IS LIKE A DUCK OUT OF WATER

HELP MAX SPLASH

Contest Rules:

- ❧ EACH AGENT WHO GETS A LISTING DRAWS A DUCK WHICH HAS AN EXTRA BIT OF CASH ATTACHED.

- ❧ NEXT, PUT YOUR NAME ON THE DUCK AND SET HIM AFLOAT IN OUR TUB OF WATER.

CONTEST RUNS FROM APRIL 1ST TO MAY 31ST

A WINNER WILL BE PICKED FROM THE TUB AND GET QUACKIN' MAX. ALSO, THE WINNING TEAM GETS DINNER AT OLIVERIO'S.

GIVING BACK TO THE COMMUNITY: INTERACTION WITH A CHARITY

Home is where the heart is and charity begins there. REALTORS® throughout America often support community causes too numerous to name. I took my lead for April's charitable work from Jack Conway and Company which covers the New England states. I was reading its monthly newsletter several years ago when I noticed an article and photographs about a "Birdhouse Extravaganza," an annual auction at which locally-designed and constructed birdhouses were sold to the highest bidder. The Conway Company donated its time and resources to sponsor this event with donations going to its partner, the Habitat for Humanity. I thought, why not do this in Morgantown too? I quickly picked up the telephone and called Jack Conway who was most gracious and delighted to share ideas, instructions and format for making a successful charitable event.

We chose our April date because the charity wanted to tie the event to gifts for Mother's Day. We nailed down a location in the common area of a local mall and began to advertise for birdhouses. I set aside money for awarding prizes in five categories: (1) functional (birdhouses to be used outside for nesting birds and beautifying backyards), (2) decorative (birdhouses for use inside as charming accents to home décor), (3) youth: grades kindergarten through sixth, (4) students: grades seven through twelve, and (5) whimsical (a "catch-all" category for fun entries which might include birdhouse-inspired jewelry, apparel, artwork, needlework, etc.)[6] We sent flyers to various schools suggesting students in art class or wood shop participate in our event. We directly contacted local craftsman and asked them to submit entries. And then we waited and waited. The silence was deafening. The entries non-existent. We worried. What if we threw an event and no one came? Since we hadn't required applications or confirmations, we had no idea what to expect. We bought birdhouses! Three days before…nothing. The day before—69 birdhouses overwhelmed us, along with a hand- made quilt with birdhouse motif. The next year—same pattern, but no panic. This time 83 entries arrived. We've been lucky with celebrity participants. Kathy Mattea and Trisha Yearwood autographed birdhouses shaped like guitars. Leslie Nielson, Priscilla Presley's love interest in Airplane! and all the spin-offs, autographed a birdhouse shaped like an airplane. We even had a birdhouse, sponsored by M&M, which was autographed by NASCAR racer Ken Schrader; the candy company also donated enough candy to be placed on the child entrants' chairs. Both years, this event generated charitable income in the range of $5,000.00 and a lot of free publicity for the charity and me.[7]

You might try doll houses, gingerbread houses or perhaps houses for Fido.

There's no reason to limit this to birdhouses. You might try doll houses, gingerbread houses or perhaps houses for Fido.

---

[6] A copy of the tri-fold program, which appears as two pages, may be found at p. 40.
[7] For photographs of the entries and event, please see pages 40-41.

GIVING BACK TO THE COMMUNITY

HABITAT FOR HUMANITY
BIRDHOUSE AUCTION AT LOCAL MALL

APRIL HEADLINES

1. No FOOLIN'
   You'll Buy When You See These Homes

2. ITEMIZE Your Needs
   We'll Find the Home to Fit Them

3. Time to INVEST

4. Don't be FOOLED
   Buy Today

5. File Jointly
   With the Deed to One of These

6. LIVE FREE
   Duplexes: Rent One, Live in One

7. Investments
   Insure Your Future Against Inflation

8. Want More IN-come
   To Offset OUT-go?
   Try These Income Properties

9. We're Out of Castles
   But We Have a Selection of Homes

10. Lock the Door Against High Rents

11. Kiss Your Landlord Good-bye

12. Long-Term Capital Gains
    Of Real Living in These Homes

13. Make April 15th Less Taxing

14. Move Your Exemptions into One of These Homes

15. One Good Investment Is Worth a Lifetime of Labor

16. Plan Your Flowerbeds in These Garden-Friendly Homes

17.   Don't Dream Too Long
        Check Out Your Future Home Today

18.   Sh-h-h-h, We Have A Secret House

19.   Say Good-bye to Rent With A Good Buy

20.   Come See, Come Sigh

21.   Don't Settle For Less
        Check With Pat

22.   Look, Linger, Buy

23.   Prime, Prime, Prime

24.   Eye-Catchers

25.   We're Having a SELLabration

APRIL Advertisements

1. "Don't Let Your Refund Get Washed Away"
   (Graphics: Dollars, labeled Tax, going down a drain)

2. "Trash or Treasure-You Decide"
   (Graphics: Rent checks hovering above a trash can and a treasure chest)

3. "Take TIME Out To Buy A New Home
   (Graphics: Lots of different types of watches)

What goes around may come around and save your life.

That first house. It's something clients dream about.

They watch videos, eat home-made popcorn and stay away from theaters. They carry bologna sandwiches instead of heading off to that quick-food joint. They walk when others ride. They "update" their basic clothing; they don't purchase the latest trendy skirt or shirt. In other words, they save, save, save.

Even with that attitude, that first house often eludes the young buyer who doesn't have folks to float a loan or that stable high-tech job that commands a handsome salary. Sometimes, they just have to rely on the kindness of strangers.

I hate it when I see a deserving couple who just can't quite make the down-payment on that new residence. Sometimes, the old softy comes out.

In May, 1990, I was diagnosed with a meningioma brain tumor which controlled my balance. I was out of kilter. I fell down a lot and I learned that it wasn't so much the fall as it was what you hit. Black and blue became my favorite colors. The tumor was the size of a walnut. The doctor feared its size might make it inoperable but we all agreed to try. Before surgery, the first step was radiation treatment to shrink the tumor's tentacles.

Prior to the operation, a doctor walked into my hospital room at University-Presbyterian in Pittsburgh, Pennsylvania to check on me. "Hi, Joe, how are you?" I asked. He replied, "I knew there could only be one Pat Stewart from Morgantown, West Virginia. I had to come and see you for myself. I'm now the Chief of Radiology here and I'll be monitoring your procedure." How ironic that this man to whom I had loaned money over 15 years earlier to buy his first home would now be guarding my life.

When the surgeon opened me up, he reported that the radiologist had been so skillful that the tumor's tentacles had pulled away from the brain's surface and rolled up into a ball. The doctor indicated that he merely reached down and plucked the tumor from my skull.

Truly the former good deed went noticed.

MAY, THE MONTH OF MOMS, GARDENS AND MEMORIALS

Temperature: It's warming up all over
Mood of the population: Making way for new housing location
Real estate climate: Couldn't be better

May is a big real estate month in this University town. Leases end on the 31st and the great housing scramble begins. Some graduating students elect to stay but must give up college housing. Other students' parents who have tired of the rental game decide buying next year's place makes more economical sense than retaining a leasehold. Faculty who are moving on look for an agent to sell the house and to refer them to a REALTOR® in that next college town. As the public school year also grinds down, families who long outgrew their houses look to find an upgrade before September rolls around.

May is a month that deserves something special. As is often the case, I found a unique idea for a new promotion in the oddest of places. In returning from Florida each Spring, we always stop at certain pre-ordained destinations. One of them is a particular highway rest stop. Outside the bathroom next to the bin filled with maps is a tourism section listing all the local haunts from caverns to trawling sites. But there are also particular brochures dedicated to the town's societies of the book and garden variety. I happened to notice that one Chapter had created a calendar and was featuring various community gardens on a daily basis. Eureka…a way to emphasize my listings by having open houses, not just on weekends but "Every Day in May." We'd show 31 houses in 31 days. We'd feature a calendar in the newspaper listing each of them. To help us defray the daily advertising cost, we partnered up with Huntington Bank who shared the costs with us. The first year of this promotion, we sold only nine or ten properties. In 2002, at least one property disappeared from our listing bank almost every day in May. In fact, it has become so popular that other REALTORS® use my promotion as leverage by pushing their customers to buy the houses before their open house dates in May.

It proved to me how closely they (my competitors) followed my advertising…

Maintaining sufficient listings for these daily openings requires a lot of work by my agents but over the years the promotion's success has led all of them to cherish obtaining their shares of the open houses. It has become part of the normal routine.

When listings are scarce, you may have trouble filling in each square on May's calendar. Get creative. Last year, we were short. One of my agents said he was bringing in a listing located in a desirable neighborhood later that day. Because we had to submit the ad before he could get the listing signed, we placed a block in the calendar's center space and called it a mystery house in a general locale. The phone rang off the hook with callers wanting to learn about the mystery. My competitors clamored to learn its address. It proved to me how closely they followed my advertising and how the ambiguous could pique the public's interest. A mystery house has now become a part of my advertising stable.

HOW TO ESTABLISH AN "EVERY DAY IN MAY" CAMPAIGN

1. Get listings. And then get more listings.

2. Sprinkle a May calendar with listings from every price range, neighborhood, and style.[8]

3. Create your ad copy for each week in May and the entire campaign.

4. Place signs in the neighborhood for the upcoming week of open houses during the week before their showing to give plenty of advance notice. For example, on the prior Tuesday, the posted sign would say "Open Monday 5-7 p.m."

5. Line up your agents for every day.

ADVERTISING THE PROMOTION

The ad campaign lasts seven weeks, two weeks more than the number of weeks in the month because it is important to give homebuyers advance notice of the daily open houses and to say thank-you at the end. The following are headlines from one year's "Every Day In May:"

1. Week before the campaign begins—
   "Pat Will Open Doors All Over Greater Morgantown in May"
   (Graphics: Pat in front of an open door)

2. Day One—
   "Open Houses: Today and Every Day in May"
   (Graphics: Calendar of May showing each open house that month)

3. Week One—
   "Pat And Her Pros: Opening Doors All Over Town
   Every Day in May: Week One"
   (Graphics: List of the open house locations for that week)

4. Week Two—
   "Hurry To Pat's Open Houses
   Every Day in May: Week Two"
   (Graphics: List of the open house locations for that week)

5. Week Three—
   "Pat's Still Opening Doors
   Every Day in May: Week Three"
   (Graphics: List of the open house locations for that week)

---

[8] For a sample calendar illustrating the layout of listings, please examine page 48.

6. Week Four—
   "Click Your Heels and Take Off To These Open Houses
   Every Day in May: Week Four"
   (Graphics: List of the open house locations for that week)

7. Week Five—   "Don't Get Locked Out
   Every Day in May—Last Week 5"
   (Graphics: List of the open house locations for the last week)

8. Conclusion of the campaign—
   "Pat Says: THANKS BUYERS
   For Making Every Day in May A Success"

This promotion is my most profitable.   May your days in May also shower profit.

MAY HEADLINES

1. Mother's Choice

2. It's Time To Buy that Gem for Mother

3. Let Pat Help You Graduate into a New Home

4. Graduate Info: A New Home

5. School's Out: Time to go House shopping

6. In MAY, You MAY
   Find the Home of Your Dreams

7. You'll Smell Like A Rose
   In Your New Home

8. Roses are Red
   Violets are Blue
   If You Have To Move
   We'll Take Care Of You.

9. YOU + HOME = Happiness

10. 5, 4, 3, 2   Pat Has A House For You
    (advertising houses with differing numbers of bedrooms)

11. Pat Studies Her Listings
    Why Don't You?

12. Make Your Heart Sing,
    Buy A New Home

13. Pat's Showcase

14. You Have Time Now To Shop For A Home

15. Purr-fect

16. Pat's Got A Lot To Show You

17. For Those Who Won't Quit And Need SEVEN Bedrooms

18.   Out-a-Ways From Town

19.   Like A Kiss From A Pretty Girl?
        Take Your Wife To See This Home

20.   North, South, East, West
        Pat Has The Very Best
        (might include compass)

May Advertisements

1.   "Capture The Magic At Pat's Place"
        (Graphics: Magician's hat with houses coming out of it)

2.   "Before You Sign Up the Truck, Sign Up Pat"
        (Graphics: Moving van)

3.   "We have the KEY to your new Home"
        (Graphics: Large Key on the side of the ad or centered under the copy)

PAT'S OPENING DOORS
EVERY DAY IN MAY!

Her Pros are waiting to greet you!

LISA PRESENTS THIS spacious country home on approximately 2 acres surrounded by stately trees with privacy galore. There are 4 to 5 bedrooms and 3 1/2 baths. $239,900.

JEFF SAYS THIS HOME has an open floor plan. A great home for entertaining. Includes decks off the back to enjoy the private setting with all the trees. $190,000.

ANNETTE SAYS PRICED TO PLEASE - BELOW APPRAISAL. Many upgrades - new roof, kitchen, gas log fireplace. Homeowners' warranty. Yours for $129,750.

LA RUE PRESENTS THIS spacious 4 bedroom home in Suncrest with separate suite on lower level. Home warranty included. Cul-de-sac. $249,900.

BB SAYS TWO HOMES and 8.032 acres for one price. Room to build more homes or just enjoy the land. Very private. Lots of room for kids to play. $450,000.

DAVID PRESENTS this 4 bedroom home with oversized garage situated on 0.74 acres. Outbuilding, above-ground pool and just 20 minutes from town. $155,000.

DO NOT DRIVE BY SAYS MARILYN, must go in to enjoy! Two bedrooms, 1 1/2 baths in old Suncrest and grounds are lovely. Hardwood floors for Oriental rugs. $119,900.

ALEX SAYS the original home is currently investment property - 3 apartments. All rented through July, 2001. $95,000.

PAT SAYS THIS modular (never lived in) is on a full foundation. Oversized one-car garage has a one bedroom apartment. Two additional lots may be purchased for $12,000. $87,000.

ANNETTE PRESENTS THIS maintenance-free home convenient to schools and hospitals. Custom designed two level decks. $120,000.

Real Estate Marketing: Pat's Way

Houses on Parade Everyday in May!!!

BB PROUDLY ANNOUNCES this stately 4 BR home on approximately 5 acres. Lots of room for children to play and located just outside of town. $299,000

MARILYN & SANDIE SAY THIS Suncrest ranch is the one you have been looking for. Nicely maintained 3 BR, 2 bath home with 25x25 FR & covered patio on level corner lot. $134,900

GUNJAN OR MARILYN WILL GREET you from this 4 bedroom brick ranch in Downwood Manor. Level house on a level lot is a miracle in this area. $159,900

BEVERLY PRESENTS THIS beautiful, well-maintained home. Special features include wainscoting in some rooms, lead cut crystal in front door, gas logs in FR & more. $94,900

BB SAYS THIS IS A GREAT LOCATION. Ranch home with lots of decking. The owners have remodeled everything in the home - new roof, kitchen, baths, septic & wiring. $149,000

PAT PRESENTS this 3 bedroom Traditional home with Old World charm, hardwood floors, sunken LR & gourmet kitchen. $279,000. Purchaser may buy an adjoining house for $54,000.

MARILYN AND SANDIE SAY nestled among tall trees, this three year old modular offers 3 bedrooms, 2 full baths, large eat-in kitchen and nice decks for your enjoyment. $79,000

PAT PRESENTS a three bedroom in Old Suncrest with professionally landscaped grounds. Fireplace and sunporch. $119,000

MARILYN SAYS finish your dream house. 2240 SF ranch under construction on approximately 9 acres. There are 3 BRs, 3 full baths, full basement. Sold "as is". $119,900

bruceton bank   Member FDIC

For finance options on all our fine properties....
Call Janet Saul, Loan Originator
at Bruceton Bank 594-2216

Check Locations! Pat's Open Homes Every Day in May!

Memories and keepsakes are the staples in June.

We graduate then.
We marry then.
We buy a home then.

We build memories then.
We treasure keepsakes then.

I come from a long line of hoarders. Perhaps, it is because I lived through the Depression. I don't know. I just don't throw anything away…except this once. Real estate cured me of my mistake.

My father, "Rounder," served in WWI, as his contemporaries used to call it. When he returned home from that great War, he packed away his uniform and helmet with pride. Despite having two brothers, I somehow became the keeper of his armed services memorabilia. As I moved from house to house over the years, I always had the uniform chest in tow. Finally, weary of the toting, I decided to donate it to the University's theater department. But, I forgot to transfer the helmet. Now, when I say tired, I mean tired. I tossed the hardhat into the trash and never looked back. As my dad advanced in years, his personal objects became more precious and I coveted every memory.

Twenty years after I'd lost contact with the uniform, I listed a cabin in the woods. On a prominent place on the wall hung a WWI helmet. "Why, my Daddy used to have one just like that," I exclaimed. To which the owner, a trash collector, responded, "no, not just like that, but exactly like that. You see I retrieved it from the garbage years ago; I knew some day I'd return it to its rightful owner." Today, it lives inside a large shadowbox in my latest home, next to photographs of him and his buddies from the War.

Sometimes the real estate business seems so one-sided. Most often, I think of REALTORS® helping others create memories in new homes. But, occasionally, if you're really lucky your customers bestow treasures on you…not just new friendships or business relationships but sometimes irreplaceable memories.

JUNE, THE "I DO" MONTH

Temperature: Heating up...in the air...in the residential sales market...in newlyweds
Mood of the population: Celebrating rites of passage
Real estate climate: The party needs a location now and is willing to pay for it.

The words "I DO" were emblazoned on a white sheet and strung between the pillars in front of her house. Why whisper it in his ear when she could shout it from the rooftop? After all, she was my agent's daughter. So, when I saw the rustling sheet as I passed Ruthie's[9] house, I wasn't surprised. I just whipped out my Polaroid and shot it. After all, this was the same agent who was known to do ballet kicks while pumping gas in order to save time. I figured the apple didn't fall far from the tree.

Although I certainly saw the humor in the photo, I did not see its potential until a number of years had passed and I decided to commemorate my anniversary with an "I DO Club" of clients taken from the sales throughout the years. After all, I decided that there is no other word duo that is more synonymous with fidelity, endurance, and substance. Like a lot of us, I'm a traditional kind of gal and I keep my promises. When my husband and I said "I do," we meant forever. This really was not much of a surprise, as both sets of our parents also eclipsed the golden 50-year mark. Longevity is, fortunately, a prominent characteristic of both my home life and business occupation. This fidelity has carried over into my professional career, leading to a current 30-year lifespan for Pat Stewart, REALTORS®. Over the years, I've taken inventory and my internal temperature to evaluate the success of my business. Along the way, I've tried to commemorate my anniversary in advertisements and with the occasional party. Since many real estate companies fail every year, I've always tried to remind my customers that I'm still in business and to instill in them an abiding belief that I'll always be around to help them.

THANK YOU, THANK YOU

My momma always taught me you can never say thanks enough to people who help you. That's especially true of people who choose you to be the one who helps them buy their most significant investment, their home. A simple hand- written thank-you card to past homebuyers gets noticed. In honor of my 30th anniversary, I sent personal notes to all of my former clients. Addressing them by their first names, I wrote: "You're members of the `I Did Buy A House From Pat Club.´ You bought your home on <u>address location</u> on June 21, 1979. I hope that this note finds you and your family in good health." Another simple, cost-effective way to remind the public of your staying power and to say "thank-you" to your agents is to have your local newspaper enlarge the number of your anniversary and imprint your agents' faces inside that integer. For example, for your third, the ad copy might contain a large three enclosing photographs and be surrounded by a headline with an anniversary theme.

---

[9]Cherished multi-million dollar seller Ruth Donaldson, who was with me for many years.

ANNIVERSARIES: CELEBRATING THE BIG ONES

For the bigger anniversary events—10, 20, 30—you may want to go all out. It's a time to invite back former agents, buyers, sellers, bankers, builders—in other words—everybody who contributed. It can get fairly pricey so be careful, and don't forget to check with the tax man. I discovered early in my career that there are companies dedicated to anniversary promotions. As my 30th anniversary in 2003 approached, I started planning my promotional themes and looking for commemorative items. As had been true in the past, Steven Fossler & Company located in Crystal Lakes, Illinois,[10] came through for me with a host of ideas. Its staff designed a 30th anniversary stamp for placement on seals to be used on correspondence, contracts and proposals. I selected Captain's chairs with the same artwork as the anniversary gift for my agents and others. A 30th anniversary banner was placed across the front of my office building.[11] All advertising for the year was tied to this 30th celebration. Since my logo, as you will recall, is the diamond, the first advertisement for the new year in the *Homes and Land Of Morgantown* magazine featured diamond rings with the headline "Ring In this 30th Diamond Anniversary in One of Pat's New Homes." Another ad incorporated a "30" and my current agents' faces. The cover of the local newspaper's property magazine in January, 2003, also showcased one of my listings and an inside story traced our company's highlights over the years. Finally, in honor of this milestone and the lasting nature of my business, I have capitalized on the stability of my client base by creating an "I DO" Club. You can do this too.

HOW TO DEVELOP AN "I DO" CLUB

This promotion is a spin-off from the garden-variety testimonials done by so many businesses. For my 30th anniversary, I gathered my yearly diaries from the recesses of basement storage and began reviewing documentation about my closings for certain special years: my first, fifth, tenth, twentieth and thirtieth years in business. After I sent out personal thank-you notes to all my former buyers, I began selecting certain people in the community who had either bought or sold houses with me and came from all walks of life. I concentrated on repeat customers and I put together a list. Then I got on the phone to contact each one of them to determine their willingness to be included in an ad. If they agreed, I followed up with a letter which required my client to sign a waiver allowing me to use their photographic likeness, name and testimonial copy without charge. My lawyer insisted. Sprinkled throughout the 30th year ad copy were former clients' photos with the caption "I Did" buy one of Pat's Homes with a date or dates of the sales and accompanied with a header, "Join the 'I DO' Club today and make one of our homes yours." This campaign demonstrates to the general public that your clients are long-term and come from all parts of the community. To add a touch of comedy to this promotion, you might also want to consider using old photographs of your clients from the years when the homes were purchased. Of course, you may make this a month-long promotion for June rather than a yearly anniversary promotion.

---

[10] Its address is 439 S. Dartmoor, Crystal Lakes, Illinois 60014, 800 no. 800-559-7374, fax. no. 800-424-9292. The company includes with its promotional items a very helpful booklet entitled, *Guide to Planning And Promoting Your Business Anniversary*.

[11] I'm a big fan of these banners. Their portability provides instant promotion for each new location, whether it be a banquet, golf tournament or picnic.

The connection between marriage and home ownership is a natural one. I was reminded of this recently when I received a phone call from an irate male voice demanding to know why I had placed a call to his residence. He'd taken my phone number off his caller-id and he wasn't buying my denial that I hadn't made such a call. He quizzed me. "Is my wife trying to sell this property without informing me? Please tell me. I thought that we'd patched up our differences but maybe I'm wrong and she wants a divorce." I couldn't put his mind to rest. As the day progressed, I couldn't put the call out of my mind either. Suddenly, it occurred to me that an oven repairman had been at my home that morning and had used my phone. I telephoned the distraught caller and asked whether he'd expected a call from a repairman. He had. He was relieved and he was so thankful for my persistence that he assured me they'd give me a call if they ever did sell the house.

While I certainly have no desire to initiate a divorce club, another all too prevalent group of prospective clients, it's clear that marital and familial status often dictate whether a new acquaintance may become a customer for your newest listing.

JUNE HEADLINES

1. Swing Into Summer

2. Summer Sizzlers

3. Say "I Do" To A New Home

4. You Don't Need To Go To The Ball Park
    To Eat "Dogs:" Add A Grill To This House

5. School's Out
    Time To Find More Play Area For The Kids

6. Take A Vacation In Your Own Back Yard

7. Hot Hot Hot Eye Stoppers

8. Graduate to the Next New Home

9. Pat's Pros Will Sweat For You

10. So Many Extras, It Will Entertain the Kids

11. It's Dad's Day
    Let Him Rest But Show Him Our Ad

12. June Is Bustin' Out All Over

13. The Diamond Dozen (13 listings—use your own logo)

14.   Fire The Landlord
       Come See Us

15.   Diamonds Are Forever
       These Gems Are Available

16.   Try These Pre-Loved Homes

17.   Pat's Pearls

18.   Pat's Pickens

19.   Give Yourself A Lifetime Gift

20.   We Have The Key To Your House

June Advertisements

Fashioning A Wedding Campaign

1. —Say "I Do" to a New Home

2. — "I Do" Take This House

3. —Be the Best Man To Buy One of These Homes

4. —We've Got the Home and the Flower Garden
       All We Need is the Wedding Party

5. —Always On Display: Doesn't Need A Red Carpet

6. —Comes With its Own Rose Petals

7. —Big Enough for the Whole Wedding Party

(Graphics: Any wedding-related items such as: rings, tiered cake, wedding gown, bridal veil)

"I Do"
Take
Pat's Homes

JANE ANN PRESENTS this 4 bedroom, 3 bath cedar home on large level lot. Front porch is a wraparound & back porch is enclosed with glass doors. $200,000.

PAT PRESENTS a 3 bedroom in Old Suncrest with professionally landscaped grounds. Fireplace and sunporch. $109,000.

SANDIE PRESENTS this well-maintained tri-level in quiet Norwood area. Walk-out in-law quarters in lower level - could be family room with full bath and second kitchen. $124,500.

BB SAYS THIS IS A GREAT location. Ranch home with lots of decking. The owners have restored everything in the home - new roof, kitchen, baths, septic & wiring. $149,000.

GUNJAN OR MARILYN WILL GREET you from this 4 bedroom brick ranch in Downwood Manor. Level house on a level lot is a miracle in this area. $159,900.

PAT SAYS there are 3 newly constructed townhomes. 2 bedrooms, complete kitchen, white tile and carpeting throughout. $119,000.

BEVERLY SAYS THIS house needs a family. It has a beautiful fenced level lot, an enclosed patio with above-ground pool, unfinished walk-up attic and a full basement. $82,000.

PAT SAYS THIS LOVELY home overlooks Cheat Lake! Boat docking privileges, great room and master suite off deck. All bedrooms open to decks. $174,999.

GLORIA SAYS TO enjoy the peace and serenity of a quiet country home! Private Cheat Lake area. $89,000.

Oops, there goes the neighborhood.

You start to worry about property value when police surround your neighbors' house and the wife's body gets carted off unceremoniously in the middle of the night. You begin to suspect that something's not quite right.

As the days pass, the sounds of auto backfire and the pop of shooting fireworks conjure visions of future mass murderers and you start to suspect foul play from everyone who's not family. This is, of course, exacerbated by the rubber-neckers doing daily rounds of the town's newest tourist attraction, the deceased neighbor's home. In hindsight, I wish I'd charged them viewing fees; I could have put all four grandchildren through college.

I digress.

Ruled a murder without a suspect, the town was in a tizzy. This is not the big city. Things like this just don't happen here…but it did. And, not just anywhere, but right across from my driveway. The speculative hum was palpable…but I tried to ignore it.

One day, a stranger arrived in my office to list some land in an adjoining county. Since we did little work in that location, I attempted to persuade him to take his listing to a closer REALTOR®. He would have none of it. As I prepared the paperwork, we began to discuss the local homicide. The more we talked, the more he shared. I learned that the time of the murder could be established by the temperature of the body and that the killer had used a .22 pistol. I began to wonder about the reasoning behind his REALTOR® selection.

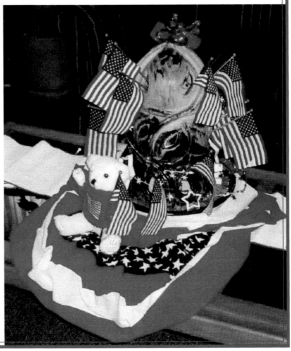

That night, I awoke from my trance convinced that the stranger had killed my neighbor. He just knew too much. Not wanting to awaken the entire household, I proceeded to write down everything I knew and posted it on the outside of the milk carton, ala missing tot style, to protect against the information loss should I get gunned down that night. My husband's constant love of cereal would save the day…and the community.

Staying up all night leads to derangement. The next morning, I was on the phone to the local prosecuting attorney, a close personal friend. I relayed the details of the stranger's conversation and learned that the caliber of weapon was accurate and had not been publicly released. I gave him all identifying information on my suspect and sent him off to investigate.

Three hours later, the impromptu probe was complete. I had "outed" a major city's Chief of Police who was in town on business.

I obviously had not helped clean up the neighborhood. Fortunately, local law enforcement was not hampered by my distractions. They merely looked to the most likely— the husband. In the upcoming weeks, he and his teen-age girlfriend (no, I do not live in Jersey) were rounded up for the pokey and a "For Sale" sign was pounded into the ground not long thereafter.

JULY, POP, ZAP, BOOM

Temperature: Lemonade-drinking, hotdog-eating, picnic weather, complete with fireworks
Mood of the population: Lazy and hazy but more than willing to buy
Real estate climate: Hot, hot, hot

An advantage to having a name like "Pat," other than having a ready-made entrée for March's annual celebrations, is its adaptability to patriotic themes around Memorial Day, Labor Day, and that grand-daddy of them all—the Fourth of July. The name produces ready headlines including admonitions to buy Pat's Patriotic Homes—they come complete with fireworks. Variations on shooting stars and the red-white-and-blue trilogy embellish my office building inside and out. While there's certainly nothing wrong with the proud placement of a few good flags on these special days, I always try to have a slight twist to the traditional decoration, even if it is merely the simple substitution of bunting for standard-flag waving.[12]

In constructing an advertisement for July, as well as for other months, a common technique is to select one emblem and place it in unexpected settings or arrangements. For example, stars are found on the American flag and cascading from the top of fireworks. If you chose this symbol for July, then the next challenge would be finding a context for its use which is appropriate to real estate sales. One suggestion might be showing a multitude of stars shooting out of a home's roof in the same manner as fireworks. In other words, the house would become the fireworks vessel and the building might be painted with patriotic colors. With those slight adaptations, the ordinary becomes less dull.

---

[12] See page 64 for photographs of exterior and interior shots of my building and the month's cover for the coffee-table centerpiece in 2002.

RACING 'ROUND TOWN

Although a significant percentage of the local population has scattered in July to unknown vacation spots, another large percentage is susceptible to the bark of the real estate sirens. This often creates a rather difficult dilemma—too many buyers for too few houses. By the time July rolls around the prior two good months of sales have frequently depleted my inventory. The challenge is to inspire already over-worked agents to find additional time to trawl for new listings. As a response to this quandary, I established a listing contest, which incited my agents to go forth and list, list, list (and refer, refer, refer).

The game goes something like this:

1. Divide your agents into 4-6 teams. You may want to consider establishing your best agents as team captains to spread the talent and having them select their team members in a revolving fashion, much like the system used on public school playgrounds throughout America in choosing a kickball team.

2. Get crafty. Purchase foam board, magic markers, checkered flags and cars. Create a large game board, much like a chart with the team designations and members running down the left axis and the number of listings and/or referrals becoming the top axis, as shown below.

3. Set up the game in a well-trafficked area in the office so that it's always on the agents' minds.

4. Draft the contest rules for the one-month competition. Mine were easy. For each listing obtained by any team member, the car advanced one space on the board. Referrals were worth a one-half space advancement. Once a team obtained a set number of listings, they crossed the finish line and entered the prize zone. For each listing in that prize zone, the team would get cash awards. With this game, all the teams could win money as long as they crossed the finish line. I established an additional reward for expensive listings with a value over a set amount. When a team member brought in one of those, he or she collected a pit pass for a "mystery prize" to be awarded at the end of the game.

5. Distribute the simple contest instructions to the participants, as shown on the next page. Allow the car to move every time a new listing or referral is brought into the office. Note: These random changes have the effect of getting everyone's competitive juices going because they have to view the game board frequently to monitor team progress.

6. Announce new listings and referrals at the weekly office meetings. This acknowledgment encourages spirited razzing in the tradition of friendly competition. Once you've followed these instructions, it's time to let the game begin. Team members, start your engines.

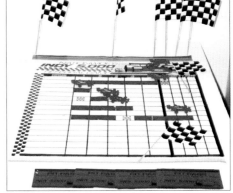

My agents seemed to love this game and the team approach for gathering listings. The office rang with good-natured ribbing from the first day of the month to the last. They yearned to solve the good old-fashioned mystery; everybody wanted a "pit pass." When I passed out the money to the winners at the end of the month and handed out two engraved Waterford pens to the pit pass winners, my agents were ready to rev up their engines again and head into August.

Pat Stewart, REALTORS®

Indy 500

Six Teams compete to win broker's surprise

**Your race car moves with a listing or with a RELO®
referral during the month of April**

Special Bonuses for faaasstt cars which get 5 listings and make it into the victory lane

**Race 1 in Victory Lane—$100
Race 2 in Victory Lane—$200
Race 3 in Victory Lane—$300
Race 4 in Victory Lane—$400**

Winning Team Wins Broker's Surprise

**Any listing over $200,000 earns a pit pass.
Place in bowl on Pat's desk—with name on
back.
Pull for Prize on May 1st**

Ladies and Gentlemen Start Your Engines!!

JULY HEADLINES

1. Pat's Sparklers

2. Don't Let Summer GO
Without Buying A New Home

3. Pat's "Pat" riotic Homes

4 Just Add the Flag Pole to This New Home

5. Hey Kids!
Want A Keen Playroom and a Short Walk to School?
Have your Parents call

6. Celebrate Independence With a New Home

7. Your Heart Will Set Off Fireworks When It Experiences These Homes

8. Light Up Your Life, Buy A New Home

9. Replace the Stars In Your Eyes with A New Home

10. Buy, Move Before School Starts

11. You Bring the Fireworks, We'll Find the Home

12. You'll Send Up Skyrockets When You See These

13. A TNT House—Trimmed, Neat and Tended

14. "Really Living!"
That's What You'll Say
When You Move In

15. Psssst: Pat Loves Buyers and Sellers

16. See 'em, Like 'em, Buy 'em

17. We're In A Tizzy Over These Houses

18. Something Good Is Always Cooking At Pat's Place

19.   POW BOOM SPLASH
Set Off Fireworks In Your New Home

20.   Front and Back: A Home Of Distinction
(show both sides of the house in ad copy)

21.   Extraordinary   Extraordinary   Extraordinary

July Advertisements

1. "Your Real Estate Hub Without the Hub Bub"
(Graphics: Wheel Spokes in the Center of a Ring of Houses)

2. "We're Headed To Pat's Place"
(Graphics: Lots of Feet)

3. "We've Got Our Eyes On A New House"
(Graphics: Photo of puppies, kittens, fish—whatever— in a box looking out)

It's August. Ah, the thrill of the vacation.

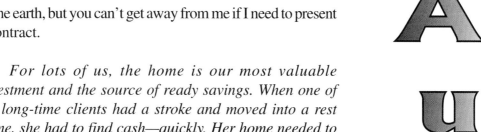

I. You can vacation at the intersection of the four corners of the earth, but you can't get away from me if I need to present a contract.

For lots of us, the home is our most valuable investment and the source of ready savings. When one of my long-time clients had a stroke and moved into a rest home, she had to find cash—quickly. Her home needed to go. We went to work and found a buyer almost immediately. The only catch was that the contract had to be approved in 24 hours or the prospective purchaser would move on to another place. No problem...I thought. But then, I discovered the daughter with the power of attorney was on vacation at a remote island off the coast of North Carolina. You know, one of those rustic, get-back-to-nature kind of places, i.e. no phone. We called their home for forwarding information. None. We called the husband's business office. They had no way to reach him. That's when knowing my customer and the family tree came in handy. We called the husband's mother. "You're in luck," she said, "they got stuck in Hurricane Felix and had to come back four days early. Sometimes, you just need a friendly evacuation or an act of God to close the deal.

II. Real estate and vacation: the perfect combination if you keep your head. But, if you don't, you may need the assistance of your favorite legislator.

I like to combine relaxation with business. That way you eliminate all guilt. No way your spouse or company associates can complain. I was attending an All Points Relocation meeting in French-speaking Quebec, enjoying both the Canadian nightlife and the informative seminars. I was using the hotel room's bar as a safe for my jewelry, most of which was short on the extravagance meter but long on the replacement value scale, as it consisted of treasured items, given to me by my husband over the years. At the conference conclusion, I made the usual hurried exit. Not until a week had passed and

I went to put on my favorite bracelet did I recall the last hiding place for my jewelry. Uh oh. And I don't speak French. After some tortured conversations with my hotel hosts, I was relieved to learn that my items had been recovered and were being mailed to me. I waited...and waited...for two weeks. Nothing. It seemed the culprit was U.S. Customs, not my fractured French. Used to seeing various items foisted off as drug smugglers' payments, the package of jewelry had been detained at the Border. Oh, brother. Now what? What had started as a relaxing visit with the Canadians sprinkled with a healthy dose of education had turned into a stressful calamity. No vacation here. Would I need to fly back? That's when I thought of Senator Jennings Randolph, a man who always had time for the foibles of his constituents. Next thing I knew, Customs was making a special delivery. A moral to this story—do not get so blinded by the restful surf and sand that you lose your mind...and all of your belongings.

AUGUST, GEE, I NEED TO GET AWAY FROM THIS PLACE MONTH

Temperature: Could it be any hotter?
Mood of the populace: Sweating—literally and figuratively in anticipation of September's crunch time
Real estate climate: Pre-school bell anxiety elicits frantic last-minute push to find new digs

Even I spend a few days at the beach during the first part of August, along with the masses on the East Coast. But I have to admit that there have been some years when I've spent as much time on the telephone straightening out contract hassles as I have frolicking in the sand. Because almost everyone in Morgantown seems to take time off in August before the college hordes return, it becomes a very compressed month, leaving fewer weeks for business consummation. Consequently, hotel fax machines get a healthy workout.

It's so busy in the real estate world this month that there is little time for special office promotions. However, there is sometimes that unusual house that screams for special attention, no matter the month, especially if it's one of those luxury homes. The key to a successful real estate business is setting yourself apart from the competition. There are so many REALTORS® today that the public has to have a good reason to pick you. One way to do that is to make your listed home an extraordinary place that everyone wants to visit. I call this the Special House Tour Promotion. It is a particularly useful tactic if you're having difficulty getting foot traffic into a particular home, Here's how you do it.

INGREDIENTS FOR A SPECIAL HOUSE TOUR

1. Take a critical look at your house and ask if there is anything about it or its owners that would set it apart from the other housing stock currently on the market. For example, if the owner was a photographer who had a gallery of his or her best photos, you might advertise the features of the house in your advertisement with a reprint of one of the owner's photos and invite the public to view the house and the homeowner's creative work.

2. Once you have selected your theme, then the fun begins by choosing those components which will highlight the property and make the open house memorable. For a pricey mansion, you might call the open house a "Top Hat Tour" or the "Caviar Express" and open the house at twilight. You could consider serving champagne or sparkling cider in stemware and appetizers or cookies on silver platters. Your agent at the open house might answer the door in a top hat which might also be featured in the advertising copy. This type of evening open house might be modified for Valentine's Day and called the Sweetheart's Rendezvous, or for any time of year, you might have evening open house hours and call it the "Buyer's Night Out." The promotion's graphics would be tailored to the particular event and might feature tuxedos and canes, softly-lit candles or just the crescent moon.

3. Tying an event to an open house presents another opportunity for innovation and family fun. If your new listing has a fabulous yard but the house is woeful, you might have a chili bake-off, a wienie roast or outdoor bingo in the yard so that prospective home buyers associate the property with fun.

SPECIAL HOUSE TOURS

A.   Things Found in A House

1.   photographs or art work
2.   clocks
3.   toy cars
4.   sports memorabilia
5.   comic books
6.   stamps or any other kind of hobby such as coins or baseball cards
7.   teddy bears or other stuffed animals

B.   Whimsical Things You Can Add to A House for Merriment Value

1.   hats or sun glasses (have visitors try them on)
2.   balloons
3.   boxes and wrapping paper
4.   mirrors (ala fun house lore)
5.   noise makers
6.   an electric train which runs through the house
7.   magician supplies and tricks demonstrated by magician

C.   Events Sponsored at a House

1. fashion show
2. bridal house—prior to June

    a.   Go into partnership with everyone needed for a traditional wedding: caterers, florists, musicians, photographers, dress makers, stores with registries
    b.   give each of the above bridal partners a separate room in the house to decorate and advertise services
    c.   tailor newspaper ad to this theme

3. baby shower house

As with the bridal house

    a.   Develop partnership with stores who sell essential items for a new baby: cribs, diapers, strollers, clothing, blankets and other bedding, toys and perhaps, financial institutions for starting various types of bank accounts for your upcoming newborn
    b.   dedicate a specific room in the house to a type of baby need or activity
    c.   tailor a newspaper ad to this theme

Note: This promotion has the additional advantage of providing your agents with a mechanism for meeting young couples in the community who will need various houses throughout their lifetimes as their families grow.

4. Meet the New Author—have a book-signing party for a new writer in your community
5. Hire an Artist to paint, a Crafts person to demonstrate crafts or a Caricaturist to do caricatures (or perhaps, all three in different rooms)
6. Come See the Belly Dancer wiggle, the body builder pose, or the gymnast tumble
7. For houses with beautiful gardens, an outdoor wine or coffee tasting open hour might draw in crowds
8. For a House with a gourmet kitchen
    a.   Hire a chef to cook some non-messy appetizers
    b.   Have a nutritionist plan a healthy diet
    c.   Allow a department store to hang kitchen gadgets throughout the house

D. Theme houses

1. Contractors' Delight
For new construction with all the bells and whistles, have all the contractors show off newest innovations

2. "Be the Best You" house
   a. Set aside room for make-up artist and a "Choose Your Colors" expert
   b. Have a fashion designer help a person dress for success
   c. Let several personal trainers give body evaluations or set up exercise plans

3. Roll out the Carpet House—have local carpet company advertise their rugs by rolling them out in different rooms in the house.

4. "Everything a Guy Ever Wanted In A House but Was Afraid to Ask For"
   a. Place antique car(s) in the yard
   b. Hang various types of hubcaps in the garage
   c. Have local home improvement store demonstrate newest power tools
   d. Invite local sports figures to sign sports memorabilia
   e. Serve barbecue and beer

You'll notice that there is one glaring thing that is absent...dancing girls. I hesitate to include those well-known pin-ups gentlemen so love to ogle. I've had experience with these props and you want to be able to get the guys out of the house some day. Several years ago, one of our clients had a teen-age son who wall-papered his bedroom ceiling in the attic with highly well-endowed lasses. My agents hated showing the house because they kept losing the men in the attic.

5. Decorate an open house with an international flair
For example, add Spanish items, rugs and food to encourage prospective clients to visit a "hard-to-sell" or "out of the way" house

E. "Giving Back Houses"

1. Invite parents to bring their kids to an open house and have a story teller or author read to the children.
2. Sponsor a craft or quilt show at an open house and have part of the proceeds go to a local charity

There is no end to the types of items, events, and themes you can use to spice up your open houses. The only limitation is your imagination.

AUGUST HEADLINES

1. You're Hot
   Get Cool
   Buy A New Home

2. This Home is Like A Beach Vacation

3. Sun Bathe On Your Own Terrace (in your own back yard)

4. Summer Is Swinging

5. It's A "NO NO"
   No Painting
   No Fixin' Up
   No Worry

6. The "HAS" House
   Has New Carpet
   Has Unbelievable Price
   Has South Park Location
   Has Extra Lot
   Has Four Bedrooms

7. "HONEY DO" House
   Honey, Do Get Your Boat Ready
   Honey, Do Plan A Party For Your Friends
   Honey, Do Lie In Bed And Eat Chocolate
   Honey, Do Call Us

8. Coming and Going
   Let Pat Help

9. Join Pat's Pros
   In Searching For A New House

10. When You Buy
    You'll Be All Smiles

11.   Instant Home: Just Add Family and Furniture

12.   Wise Old OWL Asks Who's
        Going To Buy These Gems?

13.   How Sweet It Is To Buy This Home

14.   Buy This Home And Sing A Happy Tune

15.   You'll Be Saying PINCH ME
        When You Move Into One Of These

16.   Just 5 (or 10 or 15) Minutes From Campus
        (or other important location in your town)

17.   Come On Over and Look At These

18.   Go World-wide With Pat
        She Can Refer You to Pros in Many Cities

19.   Pat Sez: "Call Me, Wontcha?"

20.   Why Wait Any Longer? Buy Now

August Advertisements

1. "We're Looking For Our New Home"[13]
   (Graphics: Line-up of the backs of babies at the beach)

2. "WANTED: All Kinds Of Property To Sell"
   (Graphics: Wanted Poster With A Picture Of A House On it)

3. "You'll Be On Target When You Call Pat's Pros
   (Graphics: Bull's Eye Target)

---

[13] The photograph for this advertisement which appears at page 72 was created for Tarbell Realty and was reprinted with its permission.

Lookin' for our new home

Pat's Pro s Will Find It!

BEV SAYS THIS Colonial home is situated on one of the largest lots in Oakview. Lot is wooded & private. Unfinished basement allows buyer to create family room or ????. $167,000

SANDIE PRESENTS THIS Four Square, 4 bedroom in South Park. Corner lot with detached 1-car garage. Close to bike trail & waterfront development area. Pocket doors. $139,900

MARILYN OR ANNETTE WILL GREET you from this 4 bedroom brick ranch in Downwood Manor. Level house on a level lot is a miracle in this area. $185,000

BB SAYS TWO HOMES and 8.032 acres for one price. Room to build more homes or just enjoy the land. Very private. Lots of room for kids to play. $450,000

LISA PRESENTS THIS spacious country home on approximately 2 acres surrounded by stately trees with privacy galore. There are 4 to 5 bedrooms and 3 1/2 baths. $224,900

SANDIE SAYS nestled among tall trees, this three year old modular offers 3 bedrooms, 2 full baths, large eat-in kitchen and nice decks for your enjoyment. $82,000

BOB SAYS timeless elegance with view of the valley. There are 9' ceilings, 4-car garage, 5 bedrooms, 4 baths and more. $375,000

DO NOT DRIVE BY SAYS MARILYN, must go in to enjoy! Two bedrooms, 1 1/2 baths, in old Suncrest and grounds are lovely. Hardwood floors for your Oriental rugs. $117,900

ALEX AND DAVID PRESENT THIS three year old home in A-1 condition. Family room on lower level. Programmable thermostat. Lots of storage. $114,900

Sellers: Rev your engines.

Football, football, football.

We may not live in Texas, but we take our pigskins seriously. Nothing interferes with THE GAME, not even real estate. Every REALTOR® has those houses that just seem to linger. Several years ago, I had such a house which had been on the market for nearly a year. I was beginning to think I'd lost the touch. That was until that one-in-a-million buyer fell in love with it and made an offer. I rushed to the telephone to contact the seller and schedule a time to present the contract. When I reached the homeowner, she told me that she couldn't meet with me because she was going to the football game. Perplexed, I stated, "Why, it's Friday. The game's tomorrow and it's here at home." She replied, "That's right. We're headed in our RV right now to the stadium parking lot to get the best tail-gating seats. We'll be back sometime on Sunday."

She didn't ask me anything about her property, not even the offered price. I'm sure she thought she had her priorities straight.

If you can't beat 'em, marry 'em.

My beloved Mountaineers play in the Big East Conference. The rivalry between the intra-Conference teams is palpable, very Hatfields and McCoys. Even the bands compete for the top position. So, it should come as

no surprise that the teams' mascots battle every game for dominance. Cross-conference students would never admit that any rival was worth his or her weight in footballs, much less courting material. That is, until two years ago.

In 2001, the game between WVU and Virginia Tech was close. The fans were riled and noisy, paying very little attention to the cheerleading squads but preferring to make up their own cheers…many of which were unmentionable. Suddenly, the OTHER team's mascot, a Virginia Tech Hokie, directed his cheerleading squad to abandon its gymnastics and cheers and pick up some special cue cards spelling out a cheer never seen before: WILL-YOU-MARRY-ME-JENNIFER? The crowd searched the stands until it discovered that Jennifer was a hometown Mountaineer, not a Hokie.

She said "yes" but he had to come to her in the rival campus town. When it came time to find a roof for their heads, they made their way to Pat Stewart, REALTORS®. We promptly found them a home where they could each find separate space, if needed, for the big game.

SEPTEMBER, BACK TO SCHOOLS AND TAIL-GATE PARTIES

Temperature: Picture perfect for everything but house-hunting
Mood of the population: Visions of textbooks and footballs dance in their heads
Real estate climate: There isn't one

I might as well go on a cruise. Everybody's too busy buying school supplies, practicing punt returns, and airing out their Fall wardrobes to give even a passing thought to changing home locations in September. Kids and sports—that's it. Because the market tends to be slow, my focus has been on getting new listings and preparing for the upcoming Oktoberfest, my second-biggest annual promotion.

Since the community's pace in September is fast-pitched, I try to invent promotions that will compete with the other activities and interest my agents. From that notion, Mountaineer Bingo was born.

MOUNTAINEER BINGO

All you need to create the "game board" for this promotion is the computer or just a piece of paper, ruler and some ink. You start out by creating a 25 square grid with five blocks on each border. The title and the color scheme for the game are from what else— football. This contest is very much like the Racing Team competition in July; however, the individual agent can win without concentrating on his or her team's antics. The key to this promotion is selecting goals which are challenging but doable and don't favor any particular agent's strengths. I like to throw in a few enjoyable, non-real estate items. The more well-rounded agent who travels in the most sectors of the community is the person who is likely to get the most listings. People turn over their homes to those they know and trust. For that reason, I include social activities on this grid. Like my other listing contests, this one also lasts for a month, awards the winners prizes but allows everyone to be a winner if he or she completes the tasks. A copy of a recent grid follows on the next page.

Mountaineer Bingo-o-o-o!!

PERSONAL BROCHURE AGENT EXPENSE	BRING 5 PERSONAL CONTACTS TO THE OFFICE	MLS DUES PAID WITHOUT BEING ASKED	CREATIVE IDEA	LISTING INVENTORY OF 5 NEW PROPERTIES
OPEN HOUSE	RENEW 2 EXPIRED LISTINGS	3 DAY WEEKEND AWAY FROM OFFICE WITH ANOTHER AGENT COVERING	MAKE 5 COLD CALLS	6 TRANSACTIONS DURING TERM OF GAME
KNOCK ON 5 DOORS FOR LISTINGS	WRITTEN GOALS FOR REST OF 2002	BOARD OF REALTOR® MEETING	PROGRAM FOR STAFF MEETING	LISTING A PROPERTY ABOVE $200,000
BECOME A NEW MEMBER OF A GROUP	LIST 2 FISBO	GREAT PERSONAL PROMOTIONAL	MET A PERSONAL GOAL	6 EMAIL ADDRESSES OF CUSTOMERS
CLEAN UP WORK STATION BEFORE LEAVING OFFICE	SENT OUTGOING REFERRAL	READ A PROFESSIONAL ARTICLE AND REPORT AT STAFF	RECRUIT A SALES AGENT	VOLUNTEER FOR A COMMITTEE ON MBOR

Rules:

The first agent to have ALL squares filled before September 30, 2002 receives $300
Second: $200
Third: $100
ANY agent who does a Cover All receives $75

As the game progresses, any agent's new listing
will be featured on WAJR Radio.

Crazy Squares

1. List 50+ acres
2. List a commercial property
3. List a $300,000 property
4. List a $400,000 property
5. Chair a Community Activity
6. Picture in newspaper
7. Six additional email addresses of customers
8. 10 hours volunteer work at your church.

SEPTEMBER HEADLINES

1. Like Blue and Gold (use your school colors)
These are winners

2. Back to School Bonus: New Home

3. Pat's De-Fense
Home Shelter

4. Winter's Coming
See Us Now

5. A Labor of Love: Pat's Homes

6. Make your Move with Pat's Pros

7. Don't Fall Behind: See Pat's Homes

8. Fall: A Beautiful Time to House Hunt

9. Fall into a House of your own

10. Move to Head of the Class, Call Pat

11. Give an "A" to These Homes

12. In a Class By Themselves

SPORTS HEADLINES

1. Who's Number One?
You Are!

2. Let us BOWL you over

3. We'll tackle your real estate needs

4. Don't be slam-dunked! See us

5. We'll hit a HOME run for you

6. Score a touchdown with your family

7.   Pat's Daily Double (when featuring two houses)

8.   Go For One

9.   We'll Bend Over Backwards For You

September Advertisements

1.   "Time's Ticking On Good Weather, See These Homes Today"
      (Graphics: Clock with spinning hands)

2.   "Bingo! Cash In Your Chips and Invest In A New Home"
      (Stacks of chips)

Sports Ads

1.   "Score a HOME in One, Call 599-9300"
      (Graphics: Putting green with flag sitting in hole with home surrounding it)

2.   "Race to This Open House"
      (Graphics: Speeding car headed toward finish line where a home sits)

3.   "You Hold the Winning Hand When You Hire Pat Stewart, REALTORS®"
      (Graphics: Poker hand showing Royal Flush)

4.   "Check Pat's Super Team For These Super Buys on This Super Sunday"
      (Graphics: Anything dealing with football)

Pat's Blue and Gold Winners!

PATRICIA A. STEWART
CRB, CRS BROKER
599-0479

PAT SAYS THIS LOVELY home overlooks Cheat Lake! Boat docking privileges, great room and master suite off deck. All bedrooms open to decks. $174,999.

JACCI SAYS there are beautiful hardwood floors, ceiling fans in all rooms, huge patio & cabana with ceiling fan & brick grill for entertaining. Nice level yard. $89,500.

IMMACULATE RAISED RANCH with Briarhill Stone and manicured grounds. Close to town & hospitals. $179,900.

BB SAYS THIS is a great location. Ranch home with lots of decking. The owners have remodeled everything in the home - new roof, kitchen, baths, septic & wiring. $149,000.

JANE ANN SAYS THIS townhouse is conveniently located to both hospitals. All appliances stay including washer and dryer. $98,500.

ALEX PRESENTS THIS 3 BEDROOM, 1 1/2 bath home in Cheat Lake. Near level yard landscaped and fenced. Home has a 1-car garage, workshop & many amenities. $75,000.

THE SUMMIT	SUNCREST AREA	MEADOWLAND
Lot 5 2 Acres	Southview Street Lot # 671 & 675	Tyrone Road 1/2 - 3/4 Acre Lots
$51,500	$89,000	$25,000 - $35,000

Member FDIC

bruceton bank

For finance options on all our fine properties....
**Call Janet Saul, Loan Originator
at Bruceton Bank 594-2216**

What's that lurking on my porch?

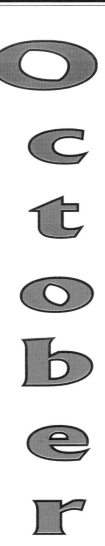

In the beginning, it had seemed like such a simple idea. He'd become the Pumpkin Man.

My son, Associate Broker Jeff Stewart, has always marched to his own cadence. Rather than sending out Christmas cards or Yuletide gifts to his clients like the masses, he has loaded up his vehicle every October. Delivering orange gourds to all of his former home buyers and sellers for Halloween has been his ticket. After all, Peter-Peter-Pumpkin-Eater also had used those orange shells as his home. What better way in the real estate world to say thanks and remember me.

It started out as a few stops every day to clients' abodes on the way home from the office. Now, it's a month-long escapade and a daily weighted-down trunk. What began when he was single is now, years later, a regular muscle-building outing for him and his two sons.

And what a promotional tool it has become. There just aren't too many people who will crawl around in the patch looking for hundreds of perfect jack-o-lanterns. Nobody gives out Halloween items in our town. So, it's memorable when a homeowner returns home to find a proud pumpkin on the stoop wearing Jeff's business card.

Last Halloween, we received a call from a homeowner wanting to know why a pumpkin had been left on his porch.

It seemed that he had recently bought the house directly from the previous homeowner and didn't know my son. When our skilled receptionist, Jodi, explained that it was just our way of saying "thanks," the caller said, "I'm new in town but have two properties for listing. You seem like the perfect REALTORS® to help me out." Throughout the years, this has been a familiar refrain.

Who's that hiding in my basement?

Some homeowners just don't get it. Before we can sell it, they have to prep it. As we all know, that means making the beds, throwing out the trash, and parting with the gaudy and useless. Old broken-down pieces of furniture are not charming antiques. Keep them at your peril.

Or our peril. Five years ago, one of my agents, Annette Drange, was attempting to show a lovely Victorian home in a respectable part of town around dusk. Upon opening the door with the original skeleton key, she discovered that most of the lights were burned out and that she and her new client had to find their way by feeling along for the next light switch. After surveying the rest of the house, they were down to seeing the basement. As they descended the stairs, it was apparent that the lower floor was dry and had been completed. Perfect. Just one last room downstairs to check. Upon opening it, they discovered an empty room which housed only a coffin with an overhead sign saying: "I was here. Sorry, I missed you." The buyer screamed, "I'm leaving. It's haunted."

When we located the owners several days later, they informed us that the coffin was merely a prop for their upcoming Halloween party. Prop or no prop, it had to go. NOW.

Why are you laughing at my dismembered finger?

Some people donate money. Others give discarded items. My spouse believes in bestowing body parts. You know, it's for science… It doesn't have to be Halloween to get a gander at a cadaver if you work at the local hospital. But, unlike the healthy screams or giggles that respond to well-placed grape eyes or spaghetti intestines, interns are charged with being respectful toward even the most withered or rotund torsos. After all, someone parted with his or her dignity in the name of learning. Hospitals don't take this adage lightly. Poking fun is a dischargeable offense.

Several years ago, following my husband's largesse of giving our most precious assets, our bodies, to the local university's hospital, I was descending in its elevator with four interns who were making fun of their latest fat and ugly specimen. As we reached the bottom floor, I turned and said, "You're going to get me one of these days and I expect respect." Horrified that their careers were over and that they had humiliated a dying patient, I watched them turn "pea green" as the doors slowly closed.

I chuckled all the way to the car.

OCTOBER, TIME TO CLEAN UP THINGS THAT GO BUMP FROM THE ATTIC

Temperature: Peas, porridge hot. Peas, porridge cold. In other words, who knows?
Mood of the population: Some are itchin' to move
Real estate climate: Surprisingly decent

By the time October rolls around, some of the town's college apartment renters have become disenfranchised with the leaky pipes and the "close-to-campus location" which requires a half-hour public transit ride and a 30-minute hike. In other words, they've discovered that the advertising was misleading and have decided to move before one more week of the school year passes. These mid-semester relocations can even move a long-standing vacant building if its location is just right.

I had been trying to sell a run-down, dreary funeral home for more than two years. Its outside just screamed, "I see dead people." The inside was no better. It was dark, dark, dark. I had asked every REALTOR® I knew how I should go about selling it in my small town. No one had a clue. Then I had my "Eureka." The upstairs would make the perfect student apartment. If I could find a commercial use for the bottom, I'd finally be able to dust off this once-proud pillared building and return it to its former glory. Fortunately, a local frequent investor shared my vision and had a college-age daughter who was looking for a place in mid-winter. In one week, the property was transformed with a whole lot of soap and a generous amount of light-colored paint. His child inherited the top. When the local Circuit Court witnessed the transformation, it leased out the rest of it. All the other local entrepreneurs were envious of the investor's bold stroke of genius.

DEVELOPING YOUR OWN OKTOBERFEST PROMOTION

In response to this mid-term migration, my broker son convinced me that progressive open houses with an Oktoberfest flavor would be the perfect companion to his pumpkin-patching habit. Out came the idea for our newest Fall promotion. The Oktoberfest is a month-long commitment to hold multiple open houses every Sunday in October during back-to-back hours in the afternoon. For example, the first open house would begin at 1:00 p.m. with others at 2:00, 3:00 and 4:00 p.m. It differs from the May promotion that features one house every day by opening multiple houses but only on every Sunday. It is set up similarly to progressive dinners where you have appetizers at the first place, salad at the next and so on. With the progressive listings, something different is featured at each place. The earliest showing might be a low-priced "starter" house while the final one featured that day might be an expensive retreat with every bell and whistle. Like my "Every Day In May," this promotion requires the full commitment of a sizeable number of agents, a larger than normal advertising budget and a big inventory of houses.

Over the years, I have been fortunate to partner on this promotion with a bank which has provided a portion of the advertising money. Each successive year, Oktoberfest has produced a greater number of sales. Splashy color ads have been a steady feature of this initiative. They begin on the last Sunday in September to herald the upcoming event, run every subsequent Sunday in October, and conclude with a "Thank you" ad the first Sunday in November. The following advertising headlines were used one recent year.[14]

The Advertising Campaign for Oktoberfest

1. Last Week in September:

It's Coming! It's Coming!
OKTOBERFEST
(Join Us for An Afternoon of Progressive Open Houses in October)

2. First Sunday in October:

OKTOBERFEST: First Sunday
Parade Around Town this afternoon with us

3. Second Sunday in October:

OKTOBERFEST: Second Sunday
Compare these houses one after the other

4. Third Sunday in October:

OKTOBERFEST: Third Sunday
These houses are good enough for Strudel

5. Fourth Sunday in October:

OKTOBERFEST: Fourth and Last Chance Sunday
Beat the trick-or-treaters to these houses

6. First Sunday in November

OKTOBERFEST Thanks You for Being Progressive

---

[14] A sample ad may be found at page 85.

Along with this advertising plan is the opportunity for differing set-ups at the houses. Here the ingenuity and creativity of your agents could dictate many options. For example, as noted before, this promotion presents the perfect time for preparing a recipe with a Halloween bent. You might try a holiday-inspired entry like pumpkin bisque, pumpkin dream bars, pumpkin bread or pumpkin crumble. A Halloween-themed centerpiece for the front entry at each of the houses is also a nice touch and leaves an unexpected calling card for the returning homeowner.

OCTOBER HEADLINES

1. No Tricks All Treats

2. No Goblins Here

3. Time For Action: Winter's Coming!

4. Boo—tiful Houses

5. Have a Boo—tiful Halloween
   Celebrate (or hide) in one of these

6. Treat Yourself to a New Home

7. Make Your Dreams Come True

8. 599-9300
   The Number To Call For Real Estate

9. So Much For So Little

10. Homes Are Flying Like Hotcakes

11. Doze In One Of These

12. Join Pat's Buyers' Club

13. You're Looking? We're Showing!

14. It's No Secret
    We Have Great Buys

15. Do Yourself A Favor
    Buy From Pat

16. Pat's Pleasing Many People
Buyers and Sellers

17. These Houses Await Your Inspection

18. Think, Then Buy

19. STARDUST Was Sprinkled On This House

20. No Fortune Teller Needed to Predict
Hours Of Family Enjoyment Here

October Advertisements

1. "I've Got Mine, Better Check with Pat for Yours"
(Graphics: Child dressed in Halloween costume in front of house)

2. "You'll Go Bats Over These"
(Graphics: Flying bats)

3. "Home Worth Seeing"
(Graphics: Photo of a pair of eyes)

4. "Sneak a Peek at These"
(Graphics: Eyes Peeking from behind a building)

It's everywhere! It's everywhere!

Some people might accuse me of doing anything to make a sale. But, I'd just tell them "real estate is everywhere." In fact, that was precisely the topic at a recent weekly staff meeting. I was discussing with my agents that I had found clients and new listings throughout the years from ordinary, every day occurrences and from the people who are stitched into the fabric of my daily life...my weekly beautician, my husband's faculty, my children's teachers. The rest of my day proved the point.

Following the meeting, I headed up the hill to one of the local hospitals to have some pesky moles removed from my back. As I was doing that medically required ritual of sitting in a cold examining room striking that most unflattering half-dressed pose, in came the nurse who told me she had decided to list her home with me in the spring. Off the table I bounded to rummage for an elusive pen to note her name and number. As I scrambled back on board, in came the doctor who had his own agenda entirely separate from my moles. "So, Pat, explain owner financing to me." As he studied my torso, I launched into a discussion of the types and advantages of his financing options.

After the procedure was completed and I was starting to get redressed, another physician stuck in his head and asked, "When are you going to sell my home?" I retorted, "Just as soon as I get dressed!"

When I returned to the office, I was giggling about the experience and relayed it to some of my agents saying, "I told you real estate is everywhere." One of them asked, "Have you got any more moles?"

November

NOVEMBER, MAY ALL YOUR TURKEYS BE ON THE TABLE INSTEAD OF AT IT.

Temperature: Baby, it's cold outside
Mood of the population: Getting ready to hibernate
Real estate climate: The days are dwindling down to a precious few

For some reason, the real estate market moves in Morgantown for the first two weeks of the month. After that, you're history until next year except for those who are looking for year-end bargains or ye olde tax dodge. People are thinking turkeys, trees and resolutions, not houses. For that reason, it's a time for taking stock, planning and picking up a new notion. You might be able to put together a seminar or two.

When the market is in full-swing, it's hard to find time to think. This is a good month for me to put some things together for the upcoming whirlwinds. While November is not a good time for a Buyer's Seminar, it's a good time to plan one for the Spring. There are so many first-time buyers who know nothing about real estate. An educated buyer is a new potential client.

PUTTING TOGETHER A HOME BUYER'S SEMINAR

1. Select a time of the year right before the crunch of the sales period. For me, the best time is April, right before my "Every Day in May" campaign or, sometimes we use the month of June.

2. Reserve a place for the seminar. While some people will tell you to get a large room, I say the cozier, the better. It makes it seem like everybody's family and I find that the interaction is better and more personal.

3. Establish a budget. My costs included those for: a) advertising, b) seminar room, c) beverage service, and d) supplies and zeroxing for the information folders. The biggest expense is your time and whole lot of energy.

4. Create program, invite speakers. My program has focused on the following presentations:
        a) why you should use a REALTOR®
        b) the value of home inspections
        c) the agency relationship for buyers and sellers
        d) financing qualifications
        e) putting together a down payment
        f) the advantages of buying versus renting, and
        g) understanding an information hot sheet

To present these topics, I chose an attorney, a home inspector, a bank loan officer, and a real estate broker. Put together advertising copy. You should have at least two ads, one on the Sunday before the seminar in the real estate section of the paper and one a day or two before the seminar.

A sample ad follows:

FREE FREE FREE	**(14 pt. Bold face)**
HOME BUYERS SEMINAR	**(18 pt. Bold face)**
Thursday Night, 7-9 o'clock	**(14 pt. Bold face)**
At the Holiday Inn	**(14 pt. Bold face)**
Pat Stewart, REALTORS® **Call 599-9300 to reserve your place.**	**(12 pt. Bold face)**

5. Set up information folders. Buy folders with pockets on both sides and a slot for a business card. My folder included: a map of the town which I have printed with my name and logo, a guide to financing options put out by the bank who was represented at the seminar, a copy of the area's Homes and Land magazine, a copy of the local newspaper's real estate magazine and a reprint of one of its articles on closing costs, and seven information sheets including, a certificate of welcome, an attendee's data sheet, an outline on the home buying process, a fact sheet on hiring a real estate attorney, and information on MLS membership, property inspections, and the pre-approval program.

Copies of some of these sample flyers follow:

Pat Stewart, REALTORS®

invites you to a <u>free</u>

home buyer's seminar

Welcome

Date: June 21, 2001

Time: 7:00 to 9:00 p.m.

Place: Holiday Inn in Star City

Pat  Stewart,
REALTORS®

Your Name _____ Work Phone _____

Home Phone _____ Fax Number _____

E-mail Address _____

Current Address _____

City/County _____ State _____ Zip Code _____

Maximum Price $ _____ Minimum Price $ _____

Minimum Square Footage (if applicable) _____

Number of People Living in Home _____

Minimum # of Bedrooms _____

Minimum # of Bathrooms _____

Garage Yes _____ No _____

Amount of Down Payment $ _____

Amount of Monthly Payment $ _____

Age of Home Preferred _____

Wooded or Open Lot Yes No _____

Subdivisions or Areas Preferred _____

_____

_____

_____

_____

School Preference _____

Driving Time/Miles to Work _____

Special Features/Comments _____

Home Buying Process

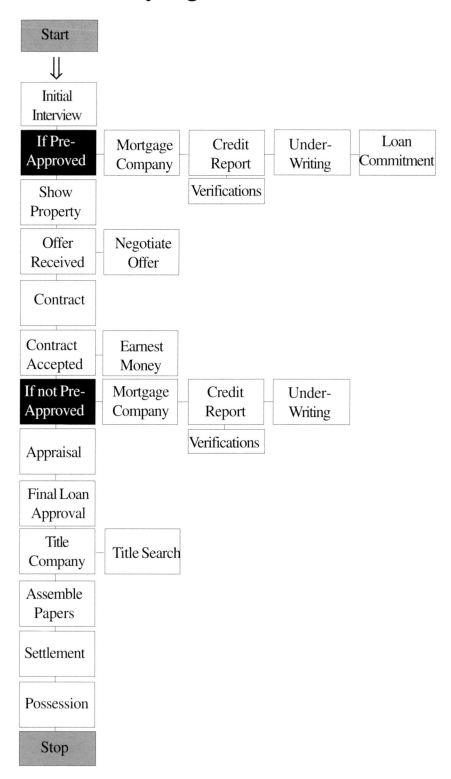

Thomas C. Stewart
Attorney at Law
2917 University Avenue
Morgantown, WV 26505
(304) 599-1850
Fax (304) 599-9303

WHY DO YOU NEED AN ATTORNEY IN A REAL ESTATE TRANSACTION?

1) An attorney is an expert that examines real estate titles to determine:

A) That the Seller has good and marketable title in the property to be sold to you. the Buyer.

B) What liens need to be satisfied prior or at the same time you are purchasing the property.

2) West Virginia is one of the few remaining "Attorney Opinion" states. which means that lending institutions have relied in the past upon an attorney's opinion to certify titles. rather than title insurance companies.

3) If you get a loan from a financial institution. the bank or mortgage company will require that you have an attorney for the aforesaid purposes.

WHOM DOES THE ATTORNEY REPRESENT IN THE TRANSACTION?

Some banks or mortgage companies are "open". which means that you may choose your own attorney. Other financial institutions don't give you a choice or don't advise you that you have a choice.

You need to ask questions at the time you make loan application. You need to ask the lender if you can choose your own attorney. Whether or not you have the right to choose your attorney, you also need to contact your attorney and ask him or her if he/she is representing you or the lender or both at the time of closing.

WHAT DOES AN ATTORNEY CHARGE?

It often depends upon the responsibilities that the attorney must complete. For instance. is the attorney closing the transaction and writing all checks or is the bank going to close the loan?

If you are allowed to choose your own attorney. you need to call around and ask attorneys for fee quotes prior to hiring an attorney. Attorneys do not have fee schedules. but you can expect to pay a minimum of $400.00 for legal services.

WHAT IS TITLE INSURANCE? WHY DO YOU NEEED IT?

It is a one-time. upfront charge to insure the lender that title to the premises is good and marketable. Title insurance may or may not be required by the lender. depending upon the type of loan you may be obtaining.

You can also purchase an owners' title insurance policy which will provide you extra coverage that an attorney can't or won't provide.

MLS Member

As a member of the Multiple Listing Service,
I can show you **any** property.

If you should see an ad in the paper
or a sign in a yard, call me to find out the
information. If you want to see it,
I'll show it to you.

Property Inspection

You can include a provision in the sales contract that gives you the right to inspect the mechanical, electrical, plumbing and structural portions of the property.

There are inspection companies that provide services of this type. You can accompany the inspector to ask question sand receive a written report itemizing any areas of concern.

If repairs are needed, you can request the seller to make them in accordance with the provisions of the sales contract.

PRE-APPROVAL PROGRAM

Many buyers are applying for a loan and obtaining approval before they find the home they want to buy.

Here are the benefits;

Your look at the "right" homes.

You save money dealing with a comfortable seller.

You close quicker.

You minimize trauma of not knowing whether or not you qualify.

NOVEMBER HEADLINES

1.   Elect Your Home Today

2.   Don't Let Another Turkey Day Go By

3.   Everything but the Turkey
Awaits in this Home

4.   It's Hunting Season for Homes Too

5.   Vote for this Winner

6.   Thanksgiving + Family + HOME = Happiness

7.   No Turkeys Here

8.   Vote for One

9.   Vote for Pat to be your REALTOR®

10.   You Will Give Thanks To Be The Proud Owner

11.   You have 61 Shopping Days Left in 200_
(descending days in subsequent ads)

12.   The Goodies Are Inside

13.   Bring Your Clothes
Everything Else Is Included

14.   Guilty, Your Honor
Of Having Real Steals

15.   WANTED: Happy Family to Enjoy This Home

16.   Call Pat To Set Up Your Personal Parade
(The photos of houses should be in a line with musical notes in between
and around them)

17.   We Can't Wait To Show These

18.   Gift-wrapped For You
(Photo of house with bow tied around it)

November Advertisements

1. "Do the Turkey Trot (In or To) One of these Homes
   (Graphics: Turkey with turkey trot footprints

2. "Elect one of Pat's Homes as Your Next Address"
   (Graphics: Voter's Ballot with voting squares next to property addresses)

3. "Add One of Pat's Pros To A List of Houses and Create One Fabulous Home"
   (Graphics: Recipe with House on it)

Do the turkey trot to one of our homes

PAT SAYS A HOME WITH ALL THE bells & whistles. What a wonderful, spacious home. 5400 SF. Could have a business downstairs & home above. $650,000.

ALEX PRESENTS THIS beautifully kept Suncrest home on a large level yard. Ranch w/2-3 bedrooms. 2 full baths & 1-car garage. A must to see. $99,900.

GUNJAN PRESENTS THIS 3 bedroom townhouse in a great location. Close to both campuses and the hospitals. Ceramic tile in kitchen. $86,900.

BB SAYS THIS IS A GREAT location. Ranch home with lots of decking. The owners have remodeled everything in the home: new roof, kitchen, baths, septic & wiring. $146,900.

GUNJAN SAYS THIS IS A GREAT LOCATION. Brick ranch with full basement. Level yard. Carpets recently replaced. Many new updates. Ready to move in. $149,900.

IMMACULATE RAISED RANCH with Briarhill Stone and manicured grounds. Close to town & hospitals. $179,900.

YOUR OWN TOP OF THE MARK IN SOUTH PARK Fantastic view. 4 bedrooms, 2 fireplaces, (2) 40' long decks. $212,500.

JANE ANN SAYS THIS townhouse is conveniently located to both hospitals. All appliances stay, washer and dryer included. $98,500.

BILL PRESENTS THIS 3 bedroom, 1 bath ranch in a quiet neighborhood. Back yard with new 10x10 storage building. Washer & dryer stays. $55,000.

bruceton bank

Member FDIC

For finance options on all our fine properties....
Call Janet Saul, Loan Originator
at Bruceton Bank 594-2216

One woman's kitchen gadget is another woman's tree ornament.

It's all in how you look at it. A well-kept, beautiful house sells itself. The trick is finding a buyer for the less than perfect homestead. The same thing holds true for most things in life. Anyone can hang tinsel and throw a bow on a Christmas tree. But decking its branches with some household-related item requires a slightly skewed sense of beauty.

Nowadays, it's not unusual to find trees dressed with almost anything but in 1973, Christmas ornaments were the only standards.

I've been hanging non-Christmas items around my real estate office during the holiday season almost from its grand opening. It started out as an economy move. The cost of those little colored balls just added up. I needed an alternative. I started out with everyday baking utensils, finding them along the way during my travels to real estate conventions. Since I wanted to be able to give one of the items to each of my sales persons and to other companies' agents who sold our listings, I needed to select well-made, colorful, inexpensive objects. Through the years, we've purchased lollipops, measuring spoons, bath muffs and powder puffs— to name a few.[15]

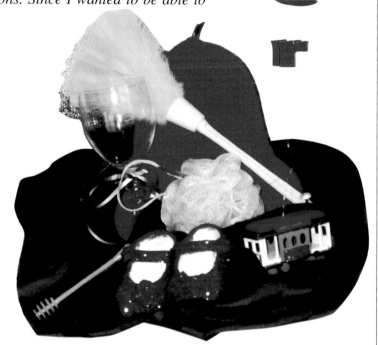

D
e
c
e
m
b
e
r

[15] Other choices included trolley cars, glass goblets with handles saying the year "2000", birds in nests, snowmen, pot holders, scrubbing massage mitts, egg timers, swizzle sticks, appetizer spreaders, gardening gloves and tools such as, tape measures and screw drivers.

In the early Fall of 1990, I attended a meeting in Toronto, Canada. Since I was always looking for the yearly tree idea, I spent time shopping for thingamajigs and doohickeys. That year, I settled on a wooden stirrer that was fond of bees. As I crossed the border into the United States, the U.S. Customs' officer asked me if I had anything to declare. "Why," I answered, "thirty honey dippers."

Again, in 1991, Toronto was my destination. I repeated the same process as before, finding my holiday memento and then packing it up for the ride home. As my spouse and I were getting ready to leave, the Customs officer inquired, "what have you to declare?" "thirty feather dusters," I responded.

He looked at me and asked, "Are you the same lady who declared 30 honey dippers last year?" "Yes, I am," I beamed. To this he retorted, "Lady, I was going to retire this year, but I'm going to have to stay around another year to see what you'll come up with next."

It was cake testers.

DECEMBER, FA LA LA AND PLAN, PLAN, PLAN

Temperature: Hunkered down but willing to divvy up the yearly profit and find one last tax investment

Mood of the population: Too busy making hot chocolate and singing carols to care

Real estate climate: Competition with sugar plums is fierce

This is the one month of the year where the external temperature has little to do with the mood in my hometown or anywhere USA. It tends to be heavy stole weather here and up and down the northern half of the East Coast. Everybody's either gathering their families close-by or heading for the nearest rowdy celebration. While I'm quite fond of the former activity, I must confess to attending the occasional unruly party.

It was during one of these gatherings at another All Points Relocation[16] convention that I misplaced that much-needed mink stole. After retracing my steps and talking to security and to the hotel manager, I returned to the place of the cocktail party and spoke to the caterer. Resorting to positive-thinking-power and the gracious understatement that we'd been discussing at the conference, I approached him and said, "I know someone who catered this party last night is really bothered because he has my stole and doesn't know how to return it to me." I asked him to check with his employees and left my name and address. Three days later, a big box containing my jacket was propped up on my West Virginia doorstep.

I do believe in those conferences and what you can learn about turning a phrase…not that it would help you all that much in December. But we do have a few customers.

Despite changes in the United States Tax Code, there are still some clients who do year-end financial inventories and look for investment properties. Consequently, my ad campaigns this month feature not only the holiday and an annual thank-you to my clients but also commercial ventures. As with both the residential and commercial real estate markets in 2003, today's exorbitant price can become tomorrow's bargain. Several years ago, one of my best clients was looking for another

---

[16] Now a part of RELO®.

commercial investment. He was already part-owner of a Las Vegas casino and decided to try his hand at Atlantic City. Using the RELO® network, I found a casino site priced at 3 million dollars. My client thought I'd lost my mind and gave up on the venture. One week later, my RELO® contact called to ask what had happened to my customer. She told me that the property had gone up in price and sold for 6 million dollars. I relayed that message to my client who fortunately enjoyed a healthy sense of humor.

While our hometown market is mercurial too, it does not soar like that in Atlantic City. My customers are pressed by the calendar and their earnings, not by the threat of uncontrollable price escalation. December is the time when I dole out awards and make my plans for the upcoming year. At the local Board of REALTORS® Christmas party every year, I give a cash award to a person who co-brokes a sale with my REALTORS®. All the co-brokers' names go into a hat[17] and a random drawing determines the winner.

Amidst the hoopla, December is a quiet time to charter new directions.

MOVING AHEAD

When we began this book, we laid out one of our most effective promotions in 2000/2001, the trail of the ruby slippers. In looking back at what made it so memorable, it seemed to come down to a generous dose of fun plus two central variables: 1) it was predicated on a story everyone knew well, and 2) it had a connection to "home." With that in mind, a new year-long promotion has been created for 2004.

NEW YEAR'S PROMOTION: THE NURSERY RHYME JINGLES

My daughter and I were sitting at the kitchen table musing about the direction of this next campaign. With the above criteria in mind, we started throwing out potential sources for providing a new theme. Fairy tales and nursery rhymes leaped to the forefront. As we each remembered our favorites, we recognized that many of them could be modified to include a real estate component. The characters poured out of us. We could use Simple Simon, Little Bo Peep, Cinderella, or the Quite Contrary Mary. We settled on fifteen ads but only your imagination limits the choices. Our selections follow:

One: That Jam-Packed Shoe

Graphics: House shaped like large shoe with tattered windows and doors and children hanging out of windows and surrounding the house

Copy: There was an old woman
Who lived in a shoe
She had so many children
She didn't know what to do
She called Pat's REALTORS® who gave her this clue
Come away with us; there's a new house for you.

---

[17]Those who co-broke with us more than once have their names placed in the hat the same number of times as the number of co-broked deals, obviously increasing their odds for the prize.

Two: He Couldn't Find the Straight and Narrow

Graphics: Crooked man by the side of crooked house on a crooked street with a crooked cat in front of the house

Copy: There was a crooked man
            Who walked a crooked mile
            He had a crooked house that didn't have much style
            He gathered up his dollars
            And he headed to Pat's Pros
            They straightened out his cat and they found a new abode.

Three: Some Children Never Sleep

Graphics: Child or toddler (running or crawling) in night clothes up or down stairs

Copy: Wee Willie Winkie running through the town
            Upstairs and downstairs in his night gown
            He's checking out the windows
            He's checking out the doors
            We'll answer all his questions and
            Do a whole lot more.

Four: At Least It Wasn't A Black Widow

Graphics: Little girl inside a house, sitting on a stool with a bowl in her lap and a spoon in her hand with a spider dangling from a web coming from above her head—perhaps have some other spiders in other parts of the house

Copy: Little Miss Muffet
            Sat on a Tuffet
            Eating her curds and whey
            Along came a spider
            Who sat down beside her
            She needed a new house today!

Five: I Know You Can You Hear Me Now

Graphics: Little boy sitting in a tight corner looking up with cell phone in his hand

Copy: Little Jack Horner
             Sat in his corner
             Looking at ceilings and floors
             He pulled out his phone
             And took out a loan
             Calling Pat to open up doors

Six: Can Anybody Stop Them From Singing?

Graphics: A group of elves carrying various kinds of household tools like screwdriver, hammer, drill and marching toward a house

Copy: Hi Ho, Hi Ho
             It's Off to Pat's We Go
             She'll Work All Day
             So We Can Say
             New Home, New Home

Seven: Some People Are Hard To Please

Graphics: House Shaped Like a Big Pumpkin with a window and door. Woman inside pumpkin with man outside

Copy: Peter, Peter, pumpkin eater
             Had a wife and couldn't keep her
             Put her in a pumpkin shell
             But there he couldn't keep her well
             He called Pat's Pros to help him out
             And n'er again did see her pout

Eight: I've Fallen And I Need A Softer Landing Strip

Graphics: A person shaped like an egg who is cracked all over and is sitting on a pile of cushions inside a house shaped like a pillow

Copy: Humpty Dumpty was cracked you see
             From a near-fatal fall out of a very tall tree
             He needed special cushions; he needed special care
             He called up Sleeping Beauty to find out who was fair
             She ushered him to Pat who called up all her Pros
             And they found a softer house and ended all his woes.

Nine: I'm Dreaming Of A White Picket Fence

Graphics: Sleeping baby smiling with a dream cloud which has a house with
picket fence in it

Copy: Hush little baby; don't you cry
Papa's gonna sing you a lullabye
He's looking for a house for your mom and you
He's asked Pat's Pros to help him make you coo
They're scouring the town and they're making choices
Next thing you'll hear will be cheerful voices.
A perfect home for the family
For Papa, and Mom and little ole me.

Ten: Help! It's Crowded In Here

Graphics: In one corner of the ad: Three men dressed like their occupations, one holding a
knife and meat, one a baker's hat with bread and the other with a cap and candles,
all of them sitting very closely in a wooden tub with slats.
In the opposite corner: three business establishments side- by-side for each
of the three professions with the 3 characters out front smiling.

Copy: Rub-a-dub-dub,
Three men in a tub,
Looking to find a place to fix grub.
One wanted two ovens
One wanted three
But one thing was certain
They all did agree
Pat's Pros were the answers
To all of their needs.

Eleven: Even Give Her Warming Drawers

Graphics: Queen in costume with hearts on her clothing in overloaded kitchen with food
everywhere and King in costume with hearts on his clothing

Copy: The Queen of Hearts
           She made some tarts,
           Some cakes, some pies, some chicken
           She looked around and then she saw
           She needed a bigger kitchen.
           The King of Hearts
           He liked those tarts,
           Those finger-lickin' dishes
           And so he asked his REALTOR®, Pat,
           To follow the Queen's wishes.

Twelve: A Peaceful Ending To A Wonderful Year

Graphics: Christmas dinner scene with angels and Santa

Copy: Christmas comes but once a year
           And when it does it brings good cheer
           A fattened goose, a child's delight
           A far-off star shining oh so bright.
           Thanks to all who bought new homes.
           To Santa, Rudolph, and his gnomes.
           Another year is round the bend
           To everyone these greetings send

Thirteen: Who's Been Sneaking Into My House?

Graphics: Child with long blonde hair surrounded by a family of bears

Copy: Goldilocks and her family always use Pat
           She Gets it J-u-s-t R-i-g-h-t

Fourteen: Pretty Is As Pretty Does.

Graphics: Big Mirror with Mom's face in it and couple standing in front of it

Copy: Mirror, mirror, on the wall,
           Who's the best REALTOR® of all?

Fifteen: I'm Tired Of Dishpan Hands.

Graphics:
Cinderella with dustpan in hand, smudged face, bent over pile of dirt
Copy:
"I'm tired of sweeping up after my sisters.
I want my own home."

The last three examples provide a fairy tale background without including lengthy copy. Thus, they require a smaller amount of ad space and are cheaper to produce.

DECEMBER HEADLINES

1.   Invest As 200__ Closes

2.   Be Home For Christmas
      and Roast Chestnuts in this fireplace

3.   Wrap One Up for Christmas

4.   Has Everything but the Gifts

5.   Go Christmas Shopping with Pat's Pros

6.   May these candles glow in your new Home

7.   A Home: The Gift for All

8.   Ho Ho Ho
      Off You Go
      (To See These Homes)

9.   Wrap Up One of These

10.   Up a tree About Christmas: Buy a New Home

11.   Santa's Choices

12. Yule Enjoy These

13. Stuff Your Stocking

14. The Perfect Gift: A New Home

15. Santa Likes These

16. Call Santa's Helpers

17. Lots Weekend

18. 24 Karat Site

19. What Are Pat's Latest Words: VIP – Very Important Properties

20. Land Ahoy!

21. Man Run Over!
    To See Commercial Investment

22. Top Drawer Opportunities

23. Don't Settle For Less
    Check Pat's List

December Advertisements

1. Thank-you ad

2. Faces of Agent as Ornaments in Tree saying Merry Xmas

3. Baby saying "Hey, bring your folks to see Pat's tree"

4. Don't tell a Soul:
   Santa Does his Christmas shopping at
   Pat Stewart, REALTORS® Or Santa Shops at Pat's Place
   (graphics: Santa)

5. Santa's face superimposed in the "O" in JOY

6. Santa Wearing Eyeglasses with a picture of a house in each lens

in one of Pat's Homes

STONEGATE
• 2 bedrooms •
1 1/2 baths
• $99,900

NORTH HILLS
2 bedrooms
• 1 1/2 baths
• $98,500

BRAVE, PA • Church Building • 2 acres • $25,000

PHILIPPI • 4 bedrooms • 2 baths • $84,000

DELLSLOW • 2 houses + 2 mobile home rentals • .6 acres • $154,000

WVU CAMPUS AREA • 2 duplexes • 3 bedrooms each • $125,000

GREEN ACRES • 3 bedrooms • 2 baths • 2+ acres • $115,000

FIRST WARD • 3 bedrooms • 1 bath • $49,900

111

Ssshhh! Don't tell a Soul ...Santa Does His Christmas Shopping At Pat Stewart, REALTORS®

BEVERLY INTRODUCES THIS well-maintained Suncrest area home. Hardwood floors, double-sided fireplace on main floor, new carpet and walk-in condition. $173,500

ALEX SAYS THE lay of the land is superb - apple trees, outbuildings and barn. Beautiful country home with 73 acres. Only 17 miles from Fairmont. $129,000

PAT PRESENTS this 3 bedroom Traditional home with old world charm, hardwood floors, sunken LR & gourmet kitchen. $289,000 Purchaser may buy an adjoining house for $54,000

GUNJAN OR MARILYN WILL MEET you at this 4 bedroom brick ranch in Downwood Manor. Level house on a level lot is a miracle in this area. $169,900

PAT PRESENTS this three bedroom townhome overlooking Cheat Lake. There are decks for your outdoor pleasure. $124,000

SANDIE'S RAISED RANCH HAS terrific space with 3 bedrooms, 2 1/2 baths in South Hills. Relax in your hot tub and let the world go by. $122,900

MARILYN & SANDIE SAY THIS Suncrest ranch is the one you have been looking for. Nicely maintained 3 BR, 2 bath home with 25x25 FR & covered patio on level corner lot. $134,900

MARILYN PRESENTS this 2240 SF ranch situated on 113 acres with woods, fields & ponds. Exterior finished. Roughed-in interior needs finished. Sold "As Is." $210,000

SUSAN PRESENTS THIS spacious 4 bedroom home with large kitchen and fenced yard. Located in Suncrest! $129,500

bruceton bank   EQUAL HOUSING LENDER   **Member FDIC**

For finance options on all our fine properties....
Call Janet Saul, Loan Originator
at Bruceton Bank 594-2216

Real Estate Marketing: Pat's Way

Ring in Pat's 30th Diamond Year!

VAN GILDER
Brick Commercial Building
Great Parking
$325,000

HIGHLAND BUSINESS PARK
Warehouse
20,000 SF on 3 Acres
$450,000

PT. MARION ROAD
4 bedrooms, 2 baths, 2 acres. $146,000

SKYLINE ESTATES
5 bedrooms , 3 baths, 2 family rooms $235,000

FAIRMONT
Senior Monogalian Building
41,000 SF on 2.5 Acres
$489,000

Garage 2200 SF on 0.4 Acres
Paint & Park Antique Cars, etc.
$74,000

CLEAN AS A WHISTLE
Car Detailing Business
Plus 3 Bedroom Home
$245,000

KIRBY EXIT
6 bedrooms, 2 1/2 baths, 18 acres. $290,000

BROOKHAVEN ROAD
Commercial Building
Apartment Above
$129,900

SOUTH PARK
4 bedrooms, 3 baths, 4 lots. $199,000

CHEAT LAKE AREA
3 Bedrooms & 1 1/2 Baths
0.75 Acres

WVU CAMPUS
2 duplexes, 3 bedrooms each. $125,000 each.

bruceton bank
EQUAL HOUSING LENDER
Member FDIC

For finance options on all our fine properties....
Call Janet Saul, Loan Originator
at Bruceton Bank 594-2216

WHAT I'VE LEARNED ALONG THE WAY

1973 to 2003: 30 years of change, some good, some bad. The stuff of history. From the avocado green and harvest gold kitchen appliances, shag carpeting, and plastic molded furniture of the 70's to chrome sub-zero refrigerators, sisal, and tufted ottoman cocktail tables of today, interiors have changed. The Rambler style is ancient history. Open, open, open floor plans are the wave of this century…now at least.

With these changes has come change in my business but along the way certain things have remained constant in the marketing game. Develop a logo

…when you're operating by the seat of your pants, turn the mundane into real estate marketing magic.

that's easy to remember and can be merged with your ads. Don't forget to say thanks and to acknowledge others as well as your anniversaries. Keep your marketing tools simple but add a touch of whimsy. With these constants in mind, I sat down last December to plan my first ad to promote my 30th Anniversary. I wanted to acknowledge the event and use my logo. Thus, the preceding diamond ring ad[18] was born. It incorporates many of the things we've discussed in this book as well as my view of style. It says thanks, it uses the diamond logo, but it places it in a ring, adding just a touch of whimsy. Finally, it acknowledges my current anniversary, taking its guidance from my principles of marketing. Cherry pits become prizes. Logs turn into alligators and pumpkins grow to be houses. In other words, when you're operating by the seat of your pants, turn the mundane into real estate marketing magic.

[18] See pp. 114-115.

ABOUT THE AUTHORS:

Patricia (Pat) Stewart got into real estate several years after the youngest of her three children headed off to school and she has never looked back. She celebrated her 30th anniversary as head of Pat Stewart, REALTORS® in 2003, and she worked for another firm for five years at the outset of her career. After the first five years she gradually built her sales force to 20 +, a level at which she has held to the present. Along the way she served as President of her local real estate board and as President of the West Virginia Association of REALTORS®. She has been an ardent member and supporter of APRS and its successor RELO®, professional real estate referral services on a national and international level. She chaired the United Way Campaign of Monongalia County, served as President of the Morgantown Chapter of Independent Fee Appraisers, President of the Morgantown Chamber of Commerce and chaired the Special Gifts campaign for the Monongalia General Hospital. She also founded the Community Newcomers Club. Moreover, she has found time to sing in her church choir.

Her formal education includes bachelor's and master's degrees from West Virginia University, Morgantown, WV.

Pat Stewart with her daughter Diane Stewart Lepley

Diane Stewart Lepley is a criminal defense attorney and civil litigator in Washington, D.C. Before setting out as a solo practitioner twenty years ago, she worked in every branch of the government starting with the United States Senate Public Works Committee where she was employed as a secretary/researcher for Senator Jennings Randolph. She then moved on to the Executive Branch where she monitored legislation for the National Bureau of Standards' Center for Building Technology and learned about the nuts and bolts of building safety. Finally, during law school, she clerked for a private civil firm and then accepted a position after graduation as Law Clerk for The Honorable Tim Murphy, Judge, D.C. Superior Court. She graduated from the University of Illinois with a B.A., from West Virginia University with an M.A. in Speech Communications and from George Washington University with a J.D.

She and her mother have been doing kooky things since they both dressed up as bunnies when Diane was five. They've decorated and concocted ad campaigns for years. This book is the latest in their joint ventures to make each other smile.

Notes

Notes

Think OUT OF THE BOX

PITS, STICKS and ALLIGATORS Workshops

Contact Pat Stewart to schedule a Real Estate Marketing workshop for your company or your local Board of REALTORS®

Spend one day with Pat and you will come away with new and innovative ideas to increase your profits. Her one-day workshop will infuse your sales team with energy and show them that creativity can be fun.

This workshop will lead your sales force in new techniques to sell property effectively in small towns and large cities.

Call for fee schedule—304-599-9300 or 800-693-5300.

Contact Pat Stewart:
Pat Stewart, REALTORS®
2917 University Ave.
Morgantown, WV 26505
pat@patstewartrealtors.com
www.PatStewartRealtors.com